Women
in India

Vedic to Modern Times

by
Susan Hill Gross & Marjorie Wall Bingham

Written under **Women In World Area Studies**, an ESEA, Title IV-C Federal Project granted by the Minnesota Department of Education.

Project Co-Directors: Marjorie Wall Bingham and Susan Hill Gross
Project Assistant: Nancy Keyt Wright

GEM
G**ARY** M**c**C**UEN**
publications inc.
411 Mallalieu Drive
Hudson, Wisconsin 54016

Photo Credits

Doranne Jacobson 10, 16, 45, 49, 56, 61
Van Gorcum 50, 52, 54
Ernest Benn 42
UNESCO 47
Royal Anthropological Institute of Great Britain and Ireland 60
Sterling Publishers Private Limited 75
University of Chicago Press 95
Wide World Photos 94
Collins Publishers 97
Uma Vasudev, from *Indira Gandhi: Revolution in Restraint* 65

Acknowledgments

Excerpts from *A Child Widow's Story* by Monica Felton, published by Victor Gollancz Ltd. Reprinted by permission of David Higham Associates Ltd.

Poem from *Women in India* by Padmini Sengupta. Reprinted by permission of the Indian Book Company.

Excerpts from *Ranade: His Wife's Reminiscences* by Ramabai Ranade. Reprinted by permission of the Publications Division, Government of India.

Excerpts from "Token Pre-Puberty Marriage in Middle India," *Journal of the Royal Anthropological Institute*, Vol. 84. Reprinted by permission of the Royal Anthropological Institute of Great Britain and Ireland.

Excerpts from *Ibn Battuta: Travels in Asia and Africa* by H.A.R. Gibb. Reprinted by permission of Routledge and Kegan Paul, Ltd.

Excerpts from *The New Brahmans* by D.D. Karve. Reprinted by permission of the University of California Press, Berkely.

Design, illustrations and typography by Richard Scales Advertising, Inc., Minneapolis, Minnesota.

GEM **publications inc.**
GARY McCUEN

411 Mallalieu Drive • Hudson, Wisconsin 54016

International Standard Book Numbers
0-86596-004-6 Paper Edition
0-86596-029-1 Library Edition

Preface

The authors of WOMEN IN INDIA wish to acknowledge the special assistance of the following people in preparing this book:

Henry Scholberg, Ames South Asian Library
Ellie Baldwin, Ames South Asian Library
Doranne Jacobson, photographs
Margo Sprague, photographs
Rosemary Johnson, editor
David Lleyveld, area consultant
Tom Crampton, pilot teacher
Gene Friesen, pilot teacher
Jerry Gottstein, pilot teacher
Gaylord Rasmussen, pilot teacher
Jack Willhite, pilot teacher
Judy Zervas, pilot teacher
Tom Egan, reader
Bert Gross, editor

In addition to these individuals, the University of Minnesota Library staff cooperated with time and patience to make research for this book possible.

Table of Contents

Introduction

WOMEN IN WORLD CULTURES is the product of a federally funded grant to develop materials on women for global studies and world history courses. The books are available in both hardback editions for library use and paper editions that may be purchased in sets of multiple copies for the classroom.

This project grew out of a search of resources which showed a clear lack of available materials appropriate for the study of women in other cultures. Women's roles in the history of various areas of the world were not included in usual curriculum and library materials. Women's lives were often subsumed under such titles as "the history of man," "the family," or "exceptional women." There were few attempts to explain or to describe how various classes of women lived at different times in particular cultures.

Cultural values were not analyzed in the context of the position of women. For example, Athens of the 5th century B.C. was usually called the "Golden Age" of Greece. Yet Athenian women had very restricted opportunities and diminished status compared to both earlier and later periods of Greek history. Materials that described Islam and the Arab world usually showed little understanding or acknowledgment of the powerful role that Muslim women often played within their "separate" worlds. In discounting the female half of humanity, the global curricular materials often seriously distorted the history and culture of these world areas.

WOMEN IN WORLD CULTURES has been designed to provide students with some resources for discovering the diversity of women's roles in a variety of world cultures. Each book presents both historical roles of women and information on their contemporary status. A major effort has been made to incorporate primary source materials. Descriptions by women of their own lives have been used whenever possible. Other types of information used include government reports, statistics, anthropologist's data, folklore, and art.

Each classroom unit includes a set of books, one teacher's guide and a sound filmstrip. A glossary of terms and a bibliography in each book aids students investigating an unfamiliar world area. The units are designed to supplement regular course offerings. The ones now available are: *Women in India, Women in the USSR, Women in Islam, Women in Israel, Women in Traditional China, Women in Modern China*. Future units include: *Women in Africa, Women in Latin America, Women in Ancient Greece and Rome, Women in Medieval and Renaissance Europe* and *Women in Modern Europe*.

Each unit has been field tested and revised to meet student and teacher comments. Students have been enthusiastic about the materials. Since these units are mainly centered around people's lives and emphasize social history, they are appealing to young people.

Chapter 1

Women in Early Indian History: The Vedas and the Laws of Manu

The caste system and complex marriage rules and rituals developed in India over a very long period of time. These customs had a profound effect on many groups of people in India. The caste system ranked people into higher and lower groups. The importance of caste and the emphasis on proper marriage with its complex wedding rituals strongly affected the position of women in Indian society. In the following section, the focus is on a shift in attitude towards women. Two early periods of Indian history will be considered. These periods are:

Vedic Period:
c. 1500–500 B.C.
Time of Manu's Laws:
c. 100 A.D.–modern times

Swayambara: Vedic woman choosing her own husband

Women in Vedic Times (c. 1500-500 B.C.)

The following is information on women in the Vedic Period. This was that long period of Indian history (c. 1500-500 B.C.) in which the Vedas or Hindu sacred texts, were composed. The Vedas[1] were oral (memorized and passed along by mouth) hymns and prayers, but indirectly included much information about daily life of the Aryans. They were conquerors from Central Europe who overran the earlier Indus Valley civilization and settled down in Northern India between 1500-500 B.C. Compared to the Indus Valley people, who lived in cities, carried on long distance trade and had a written language, the Aryans were warlike, but pastoral, tribal peoples.

Their greatest cultural contribution was the Vedas which the Aryans composed and passed along orally as they had no written language. The following information suggests the rights and privileges of Aryan women in the Vedas. The way the composer of the Vedas spoke about women gives us clues about the status of women during earlier Aryan (Vedic) times.

Following these selections from the Vedas are listed some of the laws of Manu. These Hindu laws were codified (written down) about 100 A.D. Although they are called the laws of "Manu," and he is considered the First Lawgiver of India, these laws are really a collection of all kinds of rules governing social behavior of individuals. The rules were devised by Brahman (Hindu) priests after the Vedic Period in Indian history. These "laws of Manu" were the basis of Indian-Hindu law and customs until reforms were slowly introduced in the nineteenth and twentieth centuries. Even though many of the laws that affect the status of Indian women have been improved, the customs or expected behavior of women is changing more slowly in contemporary India.

Read over the selections from the Vedas and the Laws of Manu. Either as individuals or in small groups, answer the points to consider following the selections.

1. The Vedas consist of about 20,000 prose units or stanzas in four books.

Vedas[2]

Religion: Hinduism

Girls went through the initiation ceremony called *Upanayana* (oop-pan-yana) –– thus, they were allowed to: repeat the mantras (prayers), study the Vedas, become "Risis" or "Sagas" who composed hymns and prayers.

Education:

"An unmarried, young, learned daughter should be married to a bridegroom who like her, is learned. Never think of giving in marriage a daughter of very young age."

Learning and teaching were done by the family. Girls as well as boys were taught the Vedas. There are about 20 examples mentioned in the Vedas of women becoming *risis* (poets) and *Brahaminas* (devoting their lives to Vedic scholarship).

Marriage:

Girls were married at 16 or 17. Neither men nor women could reach "heaven" after death if they were not married.

Freedom of Movement:

Girls were allowed to mingle with boys in public. They freely attended the festivals called "Samanas."

"Wives and maidens attire themselves in gay robes and set forth to the joyous feast; youths and girls hasten to the meadow forest and field...to take part in the dance. Cymbals sound, and seizing each other lads and damsels whirl about until the ground vibrates and clouds of dust envelop the gaily moving throng."

Freedom of Choice:

Boys and girls had, with the approval of their parents, a choice of marriage partner and a chance to meet young men and women. The following quotation seems to suggest that the proposal of marriage came from the individuals themselves and was not arranged by their parents.

"Become thou my partner, as thou hast passed all the seven steps with me and apart from thee I cannot live. Apart from me do thou not live."

As Wife:

The Aryans were patriarchal. The father was head of the family, but the wife had control over her household, was called "Sahadharmini" (Saha-duhrm-e-ne) [friend] of her husband and was expected to take part in the "vidatha" (vit-ah-tah) or popular government assembly.[3] Husband and wife worked as equal partners.

As Widows:

Women were allowed to remarry if their husbands died. Especially common was the custom of the widow's marrying her husband's younger brother (levirate) or of having children by the husband's younger brother without a formal remarriage (Niyoga). Regular remarriage outside her husband's family also is mentioned in the Vedas.

As Mother:

A mother is called "Matr"–– both parents "matara". The mother was held in very high respect and her status rose depending on the number of children she had.

"With sons and daughters by their side they (Aryans) reach their full extent of life, both decked with ornaments of gold."

2. The excerpts from the Vedas (in dark print) in this selection are from: Bhagwat Saran Upadhyaya, *Women in Rigveda* (New Delhi: S. Chand & Co., Ltd. 1974), Ram Nagar, New Delhi, India. pp. 179–180, 55–56; 213; 161.
3. *Ibid.*, p. 157.

A modern Brahman couple are being guided through the ancient wedding
ceremony by the village priest and barber

The Laws of Manu[4]

It is the nature of women to seduce men in this world; for that reason the wise are never unguarded in the company of females.

For women are able to lead astray in this world not only a fool, but even a learned man, and to make him a slave of desire and anger.

Women must be honored and adorned by their fathers, brothers, husbands, and brother-in-law, who desire their own welfare.

Where women are honored, there the gods are pleased; but where they are not honored, no sacred rite yields rewards.

Hence men who seek their own welfare should always honor women on holidays and festivals with gifts of ornaments, clothes, and dainty food.

If the wife is radiant with beauty, the whole house is bright; but if she is destitute of beauty, all will appear dismal.

No sacrifice, no vow, no fast must be performed by women apart from their husbands; if a wife obeys her husband, she will for that reason alone be exalted in heaven.

A faithful wife, who desires to dwell after death with her husband, must never do anything that might displease him who took her hand, married her whether he be alive or dead.

At her pleasure let her emaciate [starve] her body by living on pure flowers, roots, and fruit; but she must never even mention the name of another man after her husband has died.

Until death let her be patient of hardships, self-controlled, and chaste, and strive to fulfill that most excellent duty which is prescribed for wives who have one husband only.

A virtuous wife who after the death of her husband constantly remains chaste, reaches heaven, though she have no son, just like those chaste men.

But a woman who from a desire to have offspring violates her duty towards her dead husband, brings on herself disgrace in this world, and loses her place with her husband in heaven.

By violating her duty towards her husband, a wife is disgraced in this world; after death she enters the womb of a jackal, and is tormented by disease as punishment of her sin.

By honoring his mother he gains this nether world, by honoring his father the middle sphere, but by obedience to his teacher the world of Brahman.

In childhood a female must be subject to her father, in youth to her husband, when her lord is dead to her sons; a woman must never be independent.

She must always be cheerful, clever in the management of her household affairs, careful in cleaning her utensils, and economical in expenditure.

Him to whom her father may give her, or her brother with the father's permission, she shall obey as long as he lives, and when he is dead, she must not insult his memory.

4. Manu's laws taken from: G. Buhler, trans., *The Laws of Manu, The Sacred Books of the East*, Vol. XXV, ed., F. Max Muller (Delhi: Motilal Banarsidass, 1886, 1964).

A twice-born man, versed in the sacred law, shall burn a wife of equal caste who conducts herself thus and dies before him, with the sacred fires used for the Agnihorta, and with the sacrificial implements.

Having thus, at the funeral, given the sacred fires to his wife who dies before him, he may marry again, and again kindle the fires.

A wife, a son, and a slave, these three are declared to have no property; the wealth which they earn is acquired for him to whom they belong.

Her father protects her in childhood, her husband protects her in youth, and her sons protect her in old age; a woman is never fit for independence.

Reprehensible is the son who does not protect his mother after her husband has died.

He who carefully guards his wife preserves the purity of his offspring.

Through their passion for men, through their natural heartlessness, they become disloyal towards their husbands, however carefully they may be guarded in this world.

By the sacred tradition the woman is declared to be the soil, the man is declared to be the seed; the production of all human beings takes place through the union of the soil with the seed.

On comparing the seed and the receptacle of the seed, the seed is declared to be more important; for the offspring of all created beings is marked by the characteristics of the seed.

A man, aged thirty years, shall marry a maiden of twelve who pleases him, or a man of twenty-four a girl eight years of age; if the performance of his duties would otherwise be impeded, he must marry sooner.

For one year let a husband bear with a wife who hates him; but after the lapse of a year let him deprive her of her property and cease to cohabit with her.

A barren wife may be superseded in the eighth year, she whose children all die in the tenth, she who bears only daughters in the eleventh, but she who is quarrelsome without delay.

The teacher, the father, the mother, and an elder brother must not be treated with disrespect, though one be grievously offended by them.

Points To Consider

According to the selections from the Vedas:

1. How were unmarried young women to act?

2. What were the duties of a wife? Widow?

3. At what age were women to marry? How was a marriage partner found for them?

According to Manu:

4. What are the qualities of the ideal or good wife?

5. What are her duties toward her husband while he is alive?

6. If she is widowed, how is she supposed to behave? What happens to her if she remarries or becomes interested in another man?

7. Under what conditions can a man have more than one wife?

8. Why do you think "Manu" tells the husband to guard his wife?

9. In what role are women supposed to be honored?

10. After reading these laws, what things do you notice about Manu's idea of the following roles:

Wife	Husband
Mother	Father
Woman	Man

11. After looking over this list, what specific ways did you find women having a higher status in the Vedic Age than in the time of Manu?

12. In what specific ways did women in Vedic times have a similar status as in the times of Manu?

Chapter 2

Complexities of Hindu Marriage

Chapter Contents

A. Introduction

"We do not have any single women. Our women are born married."

This is how the Indian patriot poet, Sarojini Naidu, summarized the expectations of Indian women in the early 20th century. What she meant was that, although Indian women might be active in many occupations until recently they were all expected to marry-- and to have children. Today there are a few well-educated Indian women who remain unmarried so they can devote their time to careers in education, medicine, and social service. However, they are still considered exceptional and there is great social pressure toward marriage for young people in India.

There are several possible reasons for this Indian emphasis on marriage, especially for young women. Until recently rural pre-industrial societies stressed the importance of marriage. However, the emphasis on marriage in traditional, rural India has seemed stronger than in even other rural societies.

A reason for this emphasis on marriage might involve the Indian caste system. Caste divisions of peoples in a system of groups, each with its own built-in value or prestige, has meant that women and men were expected to marry into the proper caste. Indian society had complex rules for proper mate selection though these rules had little to do with individual choice. These complex rules can partly be traced to the Indian caste system and to the social pressures to marry within caste. Although the caste system is slowly breaking down in India, it is still a powerful consideration when selecting a marriage partner. Therefore, because the caste system made selection of proper mates

difficult, Indian parents often became obsessed with finding their children, especially their daughters, proper marriage partners.

In addition to caste considerations, Indian Hindu customs having to do with purity and pollution also focused attention on proper mate selections. Indians, especially Hindus, believe that some contacts are "polluting" or destructive while others are pure and good. For example, high caste Hindus might consider themselves polluted if they accepted food from or ate with a low caste Hindu. Only the lowest castes do certain tasks which are polluting when done by higher castes. For example, attendants or midwives at births were from the lowest castes.

Many polluting or destructive contacts might involve interaction of higher with lower castes. Many others involve contacts between men and women. For example, a woman who is having her menstrual period cannot cook food for her family and sleeps in a separate room from her husband. She would "pollute" him or her family with close contact. Widows have also been considered "bad luck" and polluting to men under various circumstances.

Sexual intercourse has been considered polluting when not properly contained within rules and marriage. This applies to young women only. They are expected to be pure sexually before marriage. Brides revealed as not being sexually pure have been rejected by their grooms and their families and returned in shame to their own families. Indian parents, then, have been very concerned with keeping their daughters pure. One way to avoid problems has been to marry

Hindu wedding ceremony.

their daughters at a young age, thus lessening the danger of contacts with young men. This pressure of keeping a daughter pure so she will not be polluting is a problem for the parents of girls.

Another problem which may contribute to the Indian emphasis on marriage for girls is the "life plan" or "dharma" that Hindus are expected to follow. Hindu "twice-born" men are supposed to follow or live out four ashramas or stages of life: studentship, householder, forest-dweller, and homeless wanderer. In the two middle stages they are to marry and fulfill family responsibilities. but during studentship and as wanderer they are instructed to live as single individuals. Though few Hindu men achieve the last two stages, the ideal high caste Hindu male spends his youth devoted to his studies (studentship stage) and would marry in his late twenties.

Hindu women have a narrower dharma to follow. As good Hindus they are supposed to marry early to produce children-- especially boy children. Boys of high caste go through the "string ceremony" when they enter the studentship stage which initiates them to adulthood. A young woman, especially of the middle class, is given a grand party after she has her first menstrual period. This is her coming of age ceremony. The gifts she receives, such as a wedding sari and kitchen tools, have to do primarily with her coming marriage. At the party she dresses as the major female gods of India and poses for pictures. She is now considered an adult and ready to have a mate found for her.[1]

In the following exercises aspects of Indian society that affect the status of girls and women are suggested. The first activity deals with the comparative value that Indian culture places on boys and girls. The second activity investigates a typical central

Indian village and some possible problems for parents in finding proper mates for their children. The third, "Wedding Rituals in Awan," may give some idea about how Indians traditionally view marriage and weddings.

1. Connie A. Jones, "Observations on the Current Status of Women in India," *International Journal of Women's Studies*, Vol. 3, No. 1 (January/February, 1980), p. 12.

B. Attitudes Toward the Sex of Children

MALE	FEMALE

Religious

MALE	FEMALE
1. Says Veda mantras (prayers) at the funeral ceremony of father.	1. Has no ceremonial role at the funeral.
2. After a father's death, only a son is able to perform rites which will salvage the father's soul and guarantee him heaven.	2. Is not allowed to hear or say the Veda mantras so she cannot say prayers for the dead ancestors.

Economic

MALE	FEMALE
1. Economic asset to family-- stays with the joint family.	1. Moves to husband's home outside of family village and will work for the husband's family.
2. Brings bride and her dowry to the family.	2. Must be provided with dowry and an expensive wedding.

Social

MALE	FEMALE
1. A son's duty is to care for parents in their old age, etc.	1. A daughter is not expected to care for elderly parents.
2. May continue living with his parents in the joint family and provide them with companionship.	2. Marries between 12-16 and moves to husband's home.
3. Not as much honor or prestige for groom's family at the wedding.	3. Great virtue brought to the family of girl when she is properly "offered as a sacrifice in marriage."
4. Chastity or sexual purity not considered as important for boys.	4. Great anxiety about her chastity (sexual purity) as she MUST be married and any rumor that she is unpure (not a virgin) will make her marriage difficult.

Points To Consider

1. What advantages do you see for having a son?
2. What advantages do you see for having a daughter?
3. About how many years does a daughter stay with her family? A son?
4. At what time in her life would a daughter be most important to her own family?
5. At what time in his life would a son be most important to his own family?

C. Hindu Marriage in Awan

The chart you just looked at on page 18 suggests that the son's role is a more lasting one to his own family than a daughter's. It also appears that marriage means a real separation of the daughter from her own family at quite an early age. However, the proper marriage of their daughter brings praise to her family. The family receiving the bride gains a dowry, worker, and potentially a future mother of additional family children.

The list below is a set of criteria or standards that are generally followed when Indian Hindus select marriage partners. On the following page is a chart showing the break-down by caste of a north-central Indian village called Awan. Awan, according to anthropologists, is typical of Indian villages in north-central India. The caste divisions and numbers of families in each caste would be similar to those found in other villages which would furnish prospective marriage partners for young people in Awan. Using the list and chart, try to answer the questions following the circular chart on caste divisions.

List of Criteria for Hindu Marriage Partner

1. A partner should be from the same caste and sub-caste (jati) or the bride *may* marry up one caste. The groom may marry *down* one caste. Remember that there are four major caste divisions or "varnas" in India.

These are (from the top down) Brahman, Kshatriya, Vaisya, and Sudra. The top three are also called "Twice Born" castes.

2. A partner must be from outside one's own village.[1]

3. A partner may not be of the same gotra (clan)... (see explanation.[2])

4. The bride's family must provide a dowry and pay for the wedding.

5. "Twice born" (top three) caste people generally will not marry widows (a woman whose husband has died)...a widower may remarry.

6. Hindus will only marry other Hindus.

7. A potential partner's physical attributes are considered. Especially important is skin color; lighter skin is considered to be a sign of higher status and beauty.

8. The partner's family is considered as to its reputation and wealth.

9. In the case of the girl, her "purity" or reputation is an important consideration. High importance is placed on chastity and virginity when a girl is considered as a marriage partner for a boy.

1. For this exercise only one village is used, as if it were two, as it is a typical village.
2. gotra=clan (group that traces to single ancestor of male line) clan=people in one's clan are usually prohibited for marriage purposes, which is one's own clan, one's father's mother's clan, one's mother's clan and one's mother's mother's clan.

D. Caste Divisions in the Village

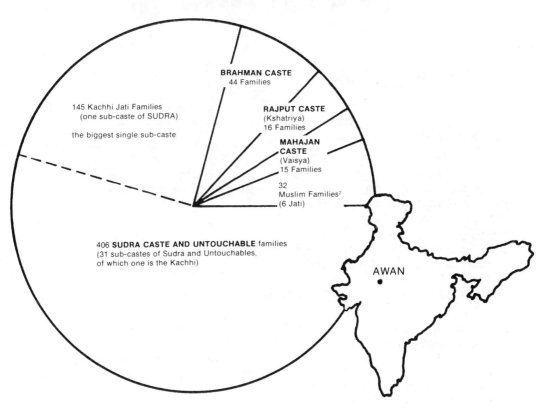

BRAHMAN CASTE
44 Families

145 Kachhi Jati Families
(one sub-caste of SUDRA)

the biggest single sub-caste

RAJPUT CASTE
(Kshatriya)
16 Families

MAHAJAN CASTE
(Vaisya)
15 Families

32 Muslim Families[2]
(6 Jati)

406 **SUDRA CASTE AND UNTOUCHABLE** families
(31 sub-castes of Sudra and Untouchables,
of which one is the Kachhi)

AWAN

Points To Consider

1. Assuming other villages have a similar caste makeup, which castes do you think would have the most difficulty finding proper bridegrooms for their daughters? List reasons for your choices.

2. In which caste do you think women have the best chances for marriage? List reasons for your answer.

3. Which families do you think might expect to receive a large dowry from the bride's family for their son's marriage?

4. Why do you think some Brahmans might reject other Brahmans as potential marriage partners even though they were from another village and had another gotra?

5. How much do you think the personal attributes of an individual would count in marriage? List some reasons for your answer.

6. A recent study says 75 percent of Indian young people still wish marriages arranged for them by their parents. Why might this be true?

1. Giri Raj Gupta, *Marriage, Religion and Society* (Delhi: Vikas Publishing House, 1974), pp. 22-40.
2. Muslims are not Hindus but followers of Muhammed and members of the religion Islam.

E. Wedding Rituals in Awan

Points To Consider

1. "Weddings are *the* grand events in [Indian] family's life."[1] What specific evidence could be offered that weddings are central to the social life of village India?

2. If weddings are such a focus of attention, what does this say about the role of marriage in Hindu life?

3. Who seems to be the center of attention in the ceremonies?

4. What groups of Indians might find it difficult to carry through these rituals? What would that say about their place in the village?

Briefly look over this list of wedding rituals, then answer the Points To Consider at the end of the exercise.

Principal Rituals Observed During the Hindu Marriage[2]

Rituals Practised in Awan	Description of Rituals Observed in Awan
1. Lagan	Sending a letter to the bridegroom's family, inviting them to solemnize the marriage.
2. Bindyak–baithana	Invocation to Ganesh deity.
3. Haladhath and snan	Assisting the bride and bridegroom to bathe, putting on new clothes and girding them with a string or rope darabha.
4. Tel-chadhana	Anointing the bride and the bridegroom.
5. Kankandora-bandhana	Tying an amulet around the wrist of the bride and bridegroom.
6. Khanagar-lana	Bringing fresh clay for plastering the house.

1. Giri Raj Gupta, *Marriage, Religion and Society* (Delhi: Vikas Publishing House, 1974), p. 78.
2. *Ibid.*, Appendix, pp. 167–171.

Saptapadi, the seven steps to happiness, in a Hindu wedding

Rituals Practised in Awan	Description of Rituals Observed in Awan
7. Chari–jhakolana	Bringing sacred water.
8. Basan–lana	Bringing new clay pots from the potter.
9. Binori	The pre–nuptial procession of the bride and bridegroom.
10. Manda–garana	Erecting a canopy where the wedding ceremonies are to be performed.
11. Pahravani	Ceremonial presentation of clothing to the parents of the bride and groom by kin and friends.
12. Agvani–karana	Honoring the bridegroom and his party on their arrival at the bride's village.
13. Ghar–dekhana	Bridegroom's going to the bride's house.
14. Badhavo–bhejana	Sending clothes and ornaments for the bride.
15. Tel–halad snan	Applying tumeric powder on the bridegroom's body from what is left over after the bride's body has been so treated.
16. Toran–marana	Reception of the bridegroom at the bride's house.
17. Grah–pravesh	The bride and bridegroom coming out into the Pandal from the inner part of the house.
18. Gath–joda bandhana	Tying tumeric pieces and betelnut on the end of the upper garments of bride and bridegroom and knotting their garments together.
19. Pani–grahana	Taking hold of the bride's hand.
20. Homa–karana	Lighting the fire and offering ajya oblations.
21. Phere	Taking seven steps together.
22. Kanyadan	Giving away the bride.
23. Sakshi–karana	Addressing the spectators with reference to the newly married bride.

Rituals Practised in Awan	Description of Rituals Observed in Awan
24. Daksina	Gifts to the Acharya.
25. Devi–devata–puja	Worship of gods and deities by the bridal couple.
26. Goran	Chief marriage feast at the bride's house.
27. Kanwar–kaleva	Offering breakfast to the bridegroom at the bride's house.
28. Milani	Meeting of the bride's kin with that of the bridegroom.
29. Jua–khelana	Ceremonial game played by the bridal couple.
30. Khetarpal–puja	Worship of the deity (protector of the village).
31. Rodi–puja	Worship of the 'Rubbish.'
32. Palangachar	Bedstead ceremony.
33. Rang–bhat	A coloured rice feast.
34. Tuntiya	Mock marriage by the women at the house of the bridegroom.
35. Barat–ki–bidai	Ceremonial farewell to the barat party.
36. Ghar–me–lena	Reception of the bridal couple at the bridegroom's house.
37. Devi–devata–puja	Worship of Siva and his consort Gauri.
38. Muha–dekhana	Showing the face of the bride to the women and the bridegroom.
39. Ratijaga	Keeping certain prohibitions for three nights after marriage.
40. Pavano–ki–bidai	Ceremonial farewell to guests.
41. Devataon–ki–bidai	Benediction to the deities and disassembling the pandal.

Chapter 3

Women's Loss of Status and Its Effects

Chapter Contents

A. Marriage Ages of Girls in India

Vedic Age (1500–500 B.C.): Girls are married at about 16 years of age.[1]

Mauryan Dynasty, followed by invasions and disorder (c. 400 B.C. – 200 A.D.): Hindu writers like Manu begin to recommend early marriages of girls, between 13 and 15.

Period before and during the Gupta Dynasty (200 A.D. – 500 A.D.): Hindu writers recommend marriage immediately after puberty -- between 11 and 13 years old.

Period of invasions and disunity (500–1000 A.D.): Prepuberty marriage now recommended -- between 8 and 10 years old.

From 1000 A.D. to British rule (1858) Recommended age for marriage is 8 or younger.[2]

The 20th Century:[3] Average ages taken from modern census figures:

Decade	Males	Females
1901–11	20.2	13.2
1911–21	20.5	13.6
1921–31	18.4	12.6
1931–41	20.2	15.0
1941–51	19.8	15.4
1951–61	21.4	16.1
1961–71	22.2	17.2

During the Vedic Age, women's position in Indian society was generally good. For many reasons a long period of decline in the status of women began in about 300 B.C. One indicator of their loss of status was the decline of the marriage age. Hindu writers, like the law giver Manu, began to recommend earlier and earlier marriages for girls. Because of early marriage their education suffered. What use was it for a family to educate a girl who would leave their home at 10 or 12 to live with her husband's family?

In the period between 700–800 A.D., the four Varnas (main castes) began to break up into hundreds of "sub-castes." Marriages were to take place only between members of the same sub-caste. Families became even

1. Marriage ages for boys generally remained between ages of 18-22 with some few caste exceptions.
2. A. S. Altekar, *The Position of Women in Hindu Civilization* (Banaras: Motilas Banarsidass, 1956), pp. 340-361
3. *Towards Equality: Report of the Committee on the Status of Women in India* (New Delhi: Government of India, Ministry of Education and Social Welfare, 1974), p. 23

Child bride (left) with older groom (right)

more anxious to find suitable husbands for their daughters and the age of marriage dropped even lower. If a girl remained unmarried, her reputation might suffer. Indian society became more and more preoccupied with the notion that girls must be "pure," be virgins, when they married. How did a family make sure that their daughters had a "pure" reputation? They married them *before* puberty at 6-10 years old.

From the fall of the Gupta Dynasty in 467 A.D. until the great Muslim Empires in the 1500's, India suffered from a series of attacks and invasions from outside and was generally disunited within. In such uncertain

times families assured the proper marriage and protection for their daughters by marrying them very young -- often to much older men. Akbar, the great Muslim emperor, tried to get rid of the custom of child marriage, but by the time of his rule, from 1556-1605, child marriage was an established tradition in India.

As you can see from the chart on page 27, child or very early marriages continued to be common in India well into our own century. Among village Indians, early marriage at 13 or 14 is still common, although by Indian law it is illegal for a girl to be married before 15.

The custom of child marriage had several bad effects on Indian women. Their education suffered. Their health suffered because of early and frequent pregnancies. Their general status declined. However, child marriages also contributed to another problem of Indian women. Because of the age differences between husbands and wives and because they were married so young, many girls became widows. Often they were widowed before they actually had lived with their husbands and consummated their marriages. In the next section we look at the problems of widows in Indian culture.

Points To Consider

1. In the Vedic Age girls were married at about 16 years of age. When is the average age of marriage again 16?

2. Between 500 B.C. and 1900 A.D. was the trend for the marriage of girls to rise or fall? What has been the trend in the 20th Century?

3. How did early marriage affect the status of Indian women? Why?

4. What were some of the possible reasons for earlier and earlier marriage of girls?

B. The Problem of Hindu Widows — "Cold Sati"

1891: 3½ times more widows than widowers

1931: 2¾ times more widows than widowers

1951: 2½ times more widows than widowers

1971: 2¾ times more widows than widowers

How might you account for the large difference in the number of widows and widowers in India?

From the time of Manu (c. 100 A.D.) widows, especially high caste Brahman widows, were expected to behave in very special ways. The customs and laws that directed their behavior became more severe as time went on. Manu allowed, although did not approve of, Niyoga[1] marriages for widows but later Hindu lawgivers prohibited any kind of widow remarriage among the higher castes. Even child widows could not remarry.

Besides suffering increased legal restrictions, widows came to be blamed for the death of their husbands. Hindus believed that a widow had committed some sin in this life or in a former incarnation (life) that had caused the death of her husband. She could make up for her sin by a strict life of prayer and self-sacrifice. By these virtuous acts she hoped to go to heaven and thereby join her husband in their next lives.

Expected behavior of widows:

1. Eat only one simple meal a day -- no honey, wine, meat, or salt -- and completely fast once a week.

2. Each month the widow's head is completely shaved by a barber.

3. A widow's time should be spent in prayer or work.

4. Her only garment is a plain, white, rough material sari -- no under-blouse, jewelry, perfume, or Tika[2] (*Tea* kah) mark.

5. A widow is never allowed to attend weddings and festivals. Widows are considered to be unlucky.

---

1. Niyoga was a custom of a widow marrying her dead husband's brother or living with him, without formal marriage, for the purpose of having heirs.
2. Tika marks are a beauty mark on a Hindu woman's forehead. Unmarried girls can use one if they choose to. Married women *always* do.

30

The child widow with her brass watering pots

The following three stories are accounts of girls who finally came to live at a special school for girls run by Ramabai (*Ram*-ah-bye), an Indian reformer of the late nineteenth century. In the first account, the widow continued to live with her husband's family after his death. The mother-in-law blamed the widow for her son's death.

"A child widow of thirteen was brought to the school by her father. She was betrothed when just emerging from babyhood, and taken to live with her mother-in-law. She never knew a child's happiness, and, when her husband died, the treatment she received became cruel in the extreme. Constantly taunted with having killed her husband by some sin committed in a former existence, starved, beaten, her body often balanced through a ring suspended from the ceiling, she became prematurely old. When her father could bear the sight no longer, and took her to Ramabai, the light had gone out of her large dark eyes, her head and shoulders were bowed as under a great burden. Ramabai's heart ached for the poor child, and she took her in. They played with her, sang to her little songs, tried to make her forget her misery, and succeeded. Soon strength returned to her limbs, the light to her eyes, and her whole expression changed as she felt the joy of being a free and happy child. She proved to be an intelligent and diligent pupil." [3]

This next girl, living with her husband's brother, was treated like a servant:

"One [girl] was married when she was five years old to a man of forty-five and she became a widow when she was six. Then she lived with her husband's brother who kept a country inn in Central India. As the child grew up, she had to do much of the work of the house. When not more than ten she was obliged, besides all the other work, to go to a well about a quarter of a mile from the house a

number of times a day to bring water in the copper jars. She carried one on her head, one on her hip and one in her hand. Then she had to wait on the guests who came to the inn, and sometimes when she had gone to bed at eleven she would have to get up because guests had come. She must get warm water for them to wash their feet, and make them comfortable. Her life was perfect misery. She tried to run away, but she did not know the country, and all she could do was to run a little way and sit down on the roadside and cry until people found her and took her home to be beaten cruelly.

"At last somebody took pity on her and took her and she was brought to our school. She remained about seven years and got an education sufficient to make her self supporting." [4]

Even though this next widow lived with her own brother, other members of the family made her life miserable:

"Y. was married when quite young and lived in an orthodox Hindu family. Her brother brought his wife to our school, but would not bring Y. because she was a widow. One of her duties was to go every morning to get water from the well. About the same time a man living next door started a business. In India it is considered unlucky for a widow to cross one's path, the work of the whole day is undone by it. So the man complained and said he would not allow it.

"One incident which she told of her life is a bit amusing. A widow is supposed to fast regularly once a week, and once a month she fasts so strictly that she is not allowed even to drink a drop of water. When the time comes for her to take her first meal she is allowed only to eat bread made of a certain kind of flour. Y. had been fasting this way and when it

3. Clementina Butler, *Pandita Ramabai Sarasvati* (New York: Fleming H. Revell Co., 1922) p. 23.
4. *Ibid.*, pp. 66-67.

A child widow of eleven with shaved head

was time for her to eat she asked her sister-in-law for some of the flour. The answer was that there was no flour of the kind in the house. Y. begged for she was very hungry but the sister-in-law after making a feint of searching said there was no flour. According to Hindu philosophy a man must not speak what is not true, but there are five cases in which he may tell a lie. One of these is that he may say what is not true to a woman. The next day Y. found a large sack of this particular flour and could not understand why her sister-in-law should have said this, but supposed it was a matter of religion and therefore all right. Later she came to our school and is so much touched by the kind way in which she is treated that she says she cannot understand why you are so kind to a widow."[5]

This next account is from a biography of a Brahman Hindu child widow, Subbalakshmi (Sue-ball-ahk-sham-e). She was married and widowed at ten. Subbalakshmi was more fortunate than most child widows. Her father, mother, and widowed aunt ('Chitty') decided that they would send her to school, not shave her head, and allow her to wear colorful saris.

The family was criticized and scolded because they broke with tradition. However, even they never considered arranging a second marriage for Subbalakshmi or allowing her to attend weddings or festivals.

In the following section, Subbalakshmi was told of her husband's death. She was not living with her husband when he died, as it was common in high caste families for the wedding to take place several years before the daughter actually left her home to live with her husband.

"Subbalakshmi had to be told about the death of her husband. Her husband had meant nothing to her, and at first the news of his death meant nothing, either. She felt nothing, because there was nothing to feel. It did not occur to her, when her mother explained what had happened, that there was any reason why she should feel sorry for herself.

"It would not have been possible, Subramania [Subbalakshmi's Father] and Visalakshi [her mother] and Chitty had agreed, to keep Subbalakshmi in ignorance of her husband's death. But they would, they decided, do everything within their power to prevent the little girl from finding out, at least until she was very much older, what it meant to be a widow. They hid their own grief. The life of the household went on as usual. No one in the family ever spoke of the dead boy whom they had never known. Even grandmother kept silent.

"It was impossible to keep visitors away. Friends and neighbors streamed into the house to offer their sympathy, to pity the little widow and to mourn with her parents over the fate that was now in store for her.

"The punishment was inescapable. Since no widow might ever, in any conceivable circumstance, be allowed to remarry, she was cut off forever from the joys of being a woman, of becoming a mother, of managing a household. From now on, most of the simple pleasures of life would be denied to her. She would no longer be allowed to attend weddings or any other kind of festivities. For a year or so, perhaps a little less or possibly a little longer, she would be allowed to dress as she did now. Then as soon as she attained her age, she would be disfigured. Her head would be shorn. She would have to stop wearing blouses, and the only garment in which she might hide her nakedness would be a sari of plain white or unbleached cotton. She would be allowed to eat only once a day, and never anything but the plainest food. Even such little luxuries as pickles and betel-nut

5. *Ibid.*, p. 67.

34

would be denied her. She would seldom go out of the house, except occasionally to visit a temple or to perform some errand that nobody else wanted to do. It would be her duty to keep, as far as possible, out of the way of other people, because even the sight of a widow was known to bring bad luck.

"She would, of course, have a home for as long as her parents lived. After her father's death her fate, as well as that of her mother and of Chitty, would depend on the attitude of the families into which her sisters eventually married. If Balam and Savitri and baby Swarnum were fortunate in their husbands, Subbalakshmi and her mother and aunt would have homes to go to in which, in return for doing a large share of household work, they would be treated kindly. Chitty who was a widow had so far been exceptionally fortunate. Most widows who had never really been wives or who had failed to become the mothers of sons were condemned to be mere household drudges, slaving away from morning till night, perpetually on the verge of starvation and with never a kind word from anybody. The most for which they might hope and pray was a happier fate in their next birth.

"Subramania and Visalakshi and Chitty succeeded, perhaps much better than they had dared to hope, in saving the little girl from hearing such talk as this. The three of them had already made up their minds that they would, somehow or other, save Subbalakshmi from her fate. They tried to save her, too, from the prying eyes and easy tears of their sympathizers. She herself, if she caught a glimpse of friends or acquaintances approaching the house would run and hide in one of the back rooms. Although she could not feel any sadness for herself, the sight of such grief made her almost unbearably miserable.

"Sometimes she failed to escape in time. One day a favourite uncle arrived unexpectedly, and walked into the room in which she was sitting. She jumped up to greet him, joyfully certain that he, at least, would be as cheerful and easy as he always was. Instead, he flung his arms around her, hugging her tightly, and burst into heaving, uncontrollable sobs. She felt his tears falling on to her face, and struggled wildly, as if he had suddenly become an enemy, to free herself. At last she succeeded, and ran out of the room. Those few minutes had been so terrible that as soon as she was alone she herself burst into agonized tears. She had not known that grown men ever wept, and the sight of her uncle's grief for her was so much more than she could bear that suddenly she, too, was sorry for herself."[6]

Before she became a widow, Subbalakshmi noticed something 'different' about the way her beloved Aunt (Chitty) dressed. Yet, she was afraid to ask why Chitty must dress in this humiliating way.

"It was about Chitty. Chitty was not old like grandmother, and although nobody had ever called her beautiful she was lovely to look at, with the kindest, merriest eyes imaginable. Yet there was something very strange in the way she dressed. Subbalakshmi's mother wore silk saris in beautiful, bright colors with nicely-made blouses underneath, and her hair was fastened in a heavy, shining knot at the back of her head. All the ladies who came to the house dressed in the same way. Only Chitty looked different. She dressed always in a sari of the plainest white cotton, with nothing whatever underneath it, so that when she was busy in the kitchen her arms were bare and her

6. Monica Felton, *A Child Widow's Story* (London: Victor Gollancz Ltd., 1966) pp. 27-29

35

Elderly widow – rough sari and shaved head

back was not properly covered. The upper edge of the sari was drawn over her head and pulled tightly around it and down behind her ears, as if she had no hair at all underneath it.

"Grandmother dressed like that, too. She was old, and perhaps that explained why. But Subbalakshmi simply could not understand why her dear Chitty, so energetic and full of fun, should be dressed in such a horrid way. Somehow, she could not tell how, she began to have a feeling that it would be wrong to ask. She had a feeling, too, that if she did ask nobody would tell her.

"She had to know. She simply had to. She was getting to be a big girl. Soon she would be nine years old. And she still could not ask."[7]

Another time Subbalakshmi observed children tormenting a child widow.

"One day when Subbalakshmi was sitting there reading, only half aware of the shouts and laughter coming from a few yards away, she was aroused by a loud, pitiful scream.

"She looked up. Seven or eight big girls were standing in a circle around a tiny tot, a baby who could not have been much more than two years old. The little creature, who had now burst into great, heaving sobs, had nothing on, not even a skirt around her waist, and the older children were laughing and teasing and making fun of her because she was a widow. Most of the other girls, Subbalakshmi could see, wore gold chains around their necks, each with a thali, the symbol of marriage, hanging from it.

"'Ha! Ha! Ha!' the big girls were shouting. 'Janaki hasn't got a thali!' They danced around her, shouting what Subbalakshmi knew was a bad word which nice people never used. 'Widow! Widow! Widow! You wicked, wicked girl not to have a thali!'

"The baby cried and cried, struggling to escape, while the dancers moved faster and faster, shouting the same words again and again. Then, at last, baby Janaki managed to slip between the arms of two of the bigger girls and ran into the house opposite.

"Subbalakshmi could see, through the unglazed window of the house, the baby's mother rush forward to pick up the child and comfort her. Then, after a minute or so, the mother took off her own thali and fastened it around her little one's neck.

"In an instant, Janaki had slipped off her mother's lap and was running out into the street again.

"The big girls were waiting. They attacked the child savagely, trying to tear the gold chain off her neck, screaming that she had no right to wear it. Janaki's mother had evidently gone back to her kitchen and was out of earshot. Subbalakshmi, half-petrified with horror, watched helplessly until the baby, still with the thali around her neck, managed to escape once more and ran into the house and disappeared.

"Subbalakshmi never saw baby Janaki again. Nor did she ever tell anyone what she had seen. She tried to put the incident out of her mind, but it kept on coming back."[8]

After Subbalakshmi is widowed she continues going to school, wearing her hair long and bright colored saris. She doesn't realize quite what it would be like to be a widow in a less progressive family until she sees their cook having her head shaved.

"During her school-days the next task was, of course, to prepare her lessons. One morning when she was sitting in her room, poring over them with her usual intentness, she chanced to look out. Through the

7. *Ibid.*, p. 19.
8. *Ibid.*, p. 21.

37

window she could see, downstairs in the courtyard, the cook, seated on a stool. Cook was a middle-aged woman who always dressed like Chitty, with her head covered closely by her sari. Now she had removed the covering. There was a short, thick stubble of greyish-black hair all over her head. A man whom Subbalakshmi knew by sight, though of course not to speak to, the barber who came to shave her father, was standing near by, holding his razor so that the blade glittered in the sunlight.

"She watched with fascinated horror, sick with disgust yet unable to turn her head away from the sight, as the man stepped forward. Barbers, she knew, were filthy, low-caste people. Their touch was polluting, even to a man, and her father always took a bath and changed his clothes as soon as he had been shaved. Yet now, though no gentleman, not even a close relative, would ever touch the hands of a lady or allow his fingers to come into contact with her garments, this dirty fellow was taking Cook's head in his hands and leaning over her as if -- as if she were not a human being at all.

"Subbalakshmi had never seen anything so horrible in her life. Did the same thing, she wondered, happen to Chitty and to other ladies who had been disfigured and who kept their heads covered? She couldn't ask. She didn't want to know.

"That morning, when she had taken her bath and changed into a fresh blouse and sari, ready to go to school, she could not eat even a mouthful of the morning meal. She said that she felt sick in her stomach, though she would not explain why. She had never guessed or imagined that anything so degrading could happen to any woman. She did not suspect, even then, that it was the quiet courage of her parents and Chitty that had saved her from a similar fate. But for days she could think of nothing else."[9]

Points To Consider

1. "Sati" was the custom of widows burning themselves on their husband's funeral pyres. Widowhood in India is sometimes called "cold Sati." What features of widowhood would make it almost like death?

2. Of the restrictions put upon widows, which would offend you the most? Which would you find the most difficult to follow?

3. If there had been a tradition for the widow to return to her own family, do you think her life would have been as difficult?

4. Why do you think that widows were not allowed to remarry and were blamed for the death of their husbands, while widowers could remarry and were not blamed for the death of their wives?

9. *Ibid.*, pp. 38-39.

C. Sati: Hero or Victim?

There is a good deal of debate among historians as to where India got the custom of *sati*[1], the burning of live widows with their dead husbands. Some claim the custom came from the Scythian[2] tradition of sacrificing members of the king's court. Others suggest the idea came from Central Asia. Still others point to the custom as being present in India as far back in history as travel accounts let us know of social customs. One famous linguist and historian, Max Mueller, claims that a mistranslation of a Rigveda text which said, "Let the mothers advance to the altar first," caused India's custom. Priests instead interpreted the text to read, "Let the mothers go into the womb of fire."[3] But whenever or how the custom of sati started, it became one of the most dramatic and later most controversial of India's social customs.

It was dramatic for several reasons. One was that the burning was staged almost as a play or drama. The woman who decided on sati was treated with great ceremony. Relatives and friends came to the house to congratulate her and to tell her messages which she was to give to their loved ones she would meet in heaven. Her hands would be dyed red so that she might make her marks on the walls of the house as a remembrance. If the family could afford it, she would be richly dressed and would ride to the site of the burning on a garlanded horse. Further ceremonies at the pyre would take

place, sometimes with the widow going around her husband's corpse seven times to the sound of the Brahman priests chanting. Then she would mount the pyre and the further ceremonies of last farewells and the giving of her valuable bracelets would occur before the flames began. The consuming fire would mark the end of the drama and the end of the widow.

The ceremonies also were dramatic because they contrasted with many other customs of Indian life. While women, especially high caste Brahman women, usually followed "purdah," the veiling of their faces, in the sati ceremonies their faces were uncovered for all to see. Also, in many places sati memorials were set up to commemorate the woman's actions. Since women were not likely to be memorialized for political or military reasons, these statues would

1. Some sources use the spelling "suttee."
2. Nomadic group in Central Europe and Russia.
3. Quoted in Edward Thompson, *Suttee*, (London: George Allen and Unwin, 1928) p. 17.

Painting of Sati

probably be a woman's only chance for fame outside of her lifetime. Another break from the usual fate of women, as the Hindu religion saw it, was that a sati might go to heaven with her husband. As a woman alone, however, her soul would need to go through more intervals to reach such an end.

The custom of sati did vary from place to place in India and in various time periods. In some places widows were buried alive or placed in deep pits so that they could not easily escape from the flames. Since polygyny (a husband with more than one wife) was practiced in some areas, it was not one wife who went into flames, but many. As late as 1842, 25 wives committed sati at the Raja of Mandi's funeral, but some writers claim hundreds may have died in former harem times. However the custom varied, it seems to have been a lasting one. Even in the early twentieth century, when sati was outlawed, reports came of "illegal actions" of widows using paraffin to burn themselves in their homes.

The Willing:
These women often impressed observers by the heroism they seemed to exhibit. The following is an account by Ibn Battuta from the fourteenth century:

"I saw three women whose husbands had been killed in battle and who had agreed to burn themselves. Each one had a horse brought to her and mounted it, richly dressed and perfumed. In her right hand she held a coconut, with which she played, and in her left a mirror, in which she looked at her face. They were surrounded by Brahmans and their own relatives, and were preceded by drums, trumpets and bugles. Everyone said to them, 'Take greetings from me to my father, or brother or mother, or friend' and they would say 'Yes' and smile at them. I rode out with my companions to see the way in which the burning was carried out. After

three miles we came to a dark place with much water and shady trees, amongst which there were four pavilions, each containing a stone idol. Between the pavilions there was a basin of water over which a dense shade was cast by trees so thickly set that the sun could not penetrate them.... On reaching these pavilions they descended to the pool, plunged into it and divested themselves of their clothes and ornaments, which they distributed as alms. Each one was then given an unsewn garment of coarse cotton and tied part of it round her waist and part over her head and shoulders. The fires had been lit near this basin in a low lying spot, and oil of sesame poured over them, so that the flames were increased. There were about fifteen men there with faggots of thin wood and about ten others with heavy pieces of wood, and the drummers and trumpeters were standing by waiting for the woman's coming. The fire was screened off by a blanket held by some men, so that she should not be frightened by the sight of it. I saw one of them, on coming to the blanket, pull it violently out of the men's hands, saying to them with a smile, 'Do you frighten me with the fire? I know that it is a fire, so let me alone.' Thereupon she joined her hands above her head in salutation to the fire and cast herself into it. At the same moment the drums, trumpets and bugles were sounded, the men threw their firewood on her and the others put the heavy wood on top of her to prevent her moving, cries were raised and there was a loud clamor."[4]

Other accounts report cheerfulness on the part of the women as they threw their bracelets to members of the crowd and sat in the flames without a trace of pain.

4. H.A.R. Gibb, Trans., *Ibn Battuta: Travels in Asia and Africa,* (London: George Routledge, 1929) pp. 191-192.

A memorial to a "Sati." The women were said to have "given arm and hand" for their husbands, thus, the raised hand. These monuments are commonplace in India and village people often worship them.

The Accepting:

Some of the widows seem to have gone to their deaths without as much spirit. Perhaps the life of "cold sati" as a Hindu widow made them unenthusiastic about continuing life, but they may not have relished a flaming end much either. The following account is by William Ward, a British observer of India from the early nineteenth century:

"By this time the pile was completed, and a quantity of straw was now spread on the top of the bed of cow-dung cakes. An increase of activity was soon visible among the men.... Mantras (prayers or incantations) having been repeated over the pile and the woman, and everything being in readiness, the hurdle to which the corpse of the husband had been fastened was now raised by six of the officiating Brahmans; the end of a cord about two yards long, attached at the other end to the head of the bier, was taken by the widow, and the whole moved slowly towards the pile. The corpse was then laid on the right side upon the straw, with which it was covered, and four men furnished with sharp swords, one stationed at each corner, now drew them from their scabbards.

"The trembling [widow] then began her seven circuits round the fatal pile, and finally halted opposite to her husband's corpse, at the left side of it, where she was evidently greatly

agitated. Here five or six Brahmans began to talk to her with much vehemence, till, in a paroxysm of desperation, assisted by the Brahmans, the hopeless widow ascended the bed of destruction. Her mother and her sister, unable any longer to sustain the extremity of their anguish, went up to the side of the pile and entreated that the horrid purpose might be abandoned; but the woman, fearing the encounter and the strength of her resolution, without uttering a word or even casting a parting glance at her supplicating parent and sister, threw herself down on the pile and clasped the half-putrid corpse in her arms. Straw in abundance was then heaped on the dead and the living; gums, resins, and other inflammable materials were thrown upon the straw which covered the bodies by one party of the Brahmans, while Mantras were repeated at their heads by the other. Six or eight pieces of kindled cow-dung cakes were introduced among the straw at different parts of the pile, ghee and inflammable materials were applied, and the whole blazed in as many places. The men with swords at each corner then hacked the cords which supported the flat canopy of faggots -- it fell and covered the lifeless corpse and the living woman."[5]

The Resisting:
Some of the widows did not wish to follow the custom of sati and depending on the caste and the historical era, made the choice to live out their lives, tending their young children or aiding the joint family. Others, however, seem not to have been given such choice and were, for a variety of reasons, literally pushed into sati. The following account is from the French traveller, Francois Bernier, who went to India in the eighteenth century:

"At Lahor I saw a most beautiful young widow sacrificed, who could not, I think, have been more than twelve years of age. The poor little creature appeared more dead than alive when she approached the dreadful pit: she trembled and wept bitterly; but three or four of the Brahmans, assisted by an old woman who held her under the arm, forced the unwilling victim toward the fatal spot, seated her on the wood, tied her hands and feet, lest she should run away, and in that situation the innocent creature was burnt alive."[6]

Points To Consider

1. Each of these three women committed sati for different motives. What would you see as the main reasons for the final fate of:

   a. The willing sati?
   b. The accepting sati?
   c. The resisting sati?

2. As in almost any action, some groups may benefit and some may lose from an event. What would you theorize might be the *benefits* or *losses* to these groups in the actions of a woman commiting sati?

   a. Persons concerned with family and caste reputation?
   b. Young children in the family?
   c. Brahman priests?
   d. Economic consideration of sons?
   e. Family affections or rivalries?

3. One modern critic of sati has claimed that the "willing sati" was more "psychologically scary" than the other two types of women. She questioned whether these women were at all heroic or whether or not they were merely the victims of society's "brain-washing." How would you see this issue?

5. William Ward, *A View of the History, Literature and Mythology of the Hindoos,* quoted in Thompson, pp. 150-151.
6. Archibald Constable (ed), *Francois Bernier: Travels in the Mogul Empire,* (London: S. Chand-Co., 1968) p. 314.

D. Infanticide

"An old Punjabi woman was asked about the birth of her first daughter. 'It was a funeral.'"

India has a lower percentage of women than men in its population.[1] This lower percentage of women may reflect a practice which has been present throughout its history: female infanticide. The killing of female babies -- or male babies -- is not alone a custom of India. Scholars have pointed to Ancient Greece and Rome, pre-revolutionary China and medieval Europe as eras in which infanticide was used with handicapped children or with what was thought to be an "excess" of girls in the family. It was, however, a custom which horrified later Christian missionaries as they came to India and one which the United Nations and the Indian government are still confronting.

For western travelers who came to India before the nineteenth century, the picture concerning female infanticide seemed a puzzling one. In certain areas, like southern India, there seemed a relative balance of the male–female population. But in other areas, like the north-central part of India, observers reported that the practice of female infanticide seemed widespread. Early statistics seem hard to trust or analyze. Purdah meant that some women might not be seen. Some families did not "count" daughters as important when asked how many children lived with them. Further, reports of infant deaths might be given only reluctantly to authorities like the British who might disapprove and investigate reports of infanticide. But some Indians were quite open to early travelers' questions concerning infanticide, saying that they never reared daughters in their families.[2] One Rajput family was found to have had no grown-up daughters for over one hundred years.[3]

Yet as the population did increase, it is apparent that some girls *were* raised. Groups which seem to have practiced more infanticide than others were generally ones who were very concerned with proper caste or ones who lived in areas with high dowry considerations. A father might give approval to the killing of a legitimate daughter while allowing an illegitimate one to live. A legitimate daughter would mean a search for a proper bridegroom and dowry which might be as high as the total family earnings for several years. The *status* of the baby, then, might have an effect on

1. *Per Thousand* Women   Men
   U.S.A.:   1054   1000
   India :   930   1000
Figures from: *Towards Equality: Report of the Committee on the Status of Women in India,* (New Delhi, Ministry of Education and Social Welfare, 1974) pp. 10, 15.
2. James Peggs, *India's Cries to British Humanity,* (London: Simpkin & Marshall, 1832), p. 28.
3. John Wilson, *History of the Suppression of Infanticide in Western India* (Bombay: Smith, Taylor, 1840), p. 73.

A family planning poster typical of India's governmental action encouraging smaller, planned families today

her survival; the higher the caste, the more problems that might be created in finding a proper husband.

The reasons for infanticide are understandable: the poverty of the people, the religious and social customs which emphasized the need for sons. Nevertheless, the reports of infanticides were very disturbing to many Western and Indian reformers. The actual details of infanticides were rather grizzly. Some reports mentioned burying the infant alive under the floor, or placing the baby where the hogs could eat it or feeding her opium or simply letting her die from neglect and lack of food.

Gradually the practice of female infanticide became less and less respectable as both the British and the later Indian governments worked to abolish it. There is still some concern in India, however, about female babies.

This picture on the next page is from a UNESCO publication showing the difference in physical health between twins, one a boy, the other a girl. The picture illustrates that even in one family the resources of food and attention may go to the male child and not the female.

Age Specific Death Rates[4]
(per thousand)

	INDIA[5]			UNITED STATES[6]			
Age	Male	Female	Age	Male White	Female White	Male Non-White	Female Non-White
0–4	58.3	70.2	0–4	21.9	16.8	41.6	32.9
5–14	4.5	5.3	5–14	0.5	0.3	0.6	0.4

Points To Consider

1. Is the UNESCO photograph a valid historical document?

2. What comparisons can be made between Indian infant rates and U.S. white children? What comparisons between Indian children and non-white U.S. children?

3. If infanticide is to be reduced, what situations do you see as needing change?

4. Statistics based on 1969-1970 Census.
5. *Towards Equality: Report on the Status of Women in India*, (Government of India, New Delhi: 1974), p. 20.
6. Ann Golenpaul, *Information Please Almanac: 1977*, (Information Please Almanac, N.Y.: 1977), p. 720.

Indian mother with twins: A girl and a boy

E. The Purdah System

"A woman is well either in the home or in the grave."[1]

The term "purdah" comes from a Persian word meaning "curtain." Among certain groups and castes in India, both Hindu and Muslim, a "Purdah System" is customary for women. Purdah is a way to enforce high standards of modesty on women, especially in their relations to men.[2] Although purdah can take many forms, it usually involves:

1. Having a special part of the house in which women live and work -- in South Asia called a zenana.

2. The complete covering of women, including the face, in the company of men and outside the zenana.

3. The placing of strict limits on the physical activities of women.

Hindu purdah usually starts for girls at marriage when they move from their home to that of their husband's. In their husband's home they are expected to cover (veil) their faces when they are in the company of the older men in the family and when they are outside. They do not do so when they visit their family's village or in front of the younger brothers of their husband. Wealthier village and city Hindus who still keep the purdah customs have a special place for women to sleep and do their work in the day time.[3]

Muslim purdah usually begins at puberty. Muslim women do not have to be veiled with male relatives, but must always be veiled outside the home. Begum Shaista Ikramullah (Ikram-ool-*la*-ah), a Muslim woman who grew up in India before Pakistan broke away to become a separate country, later became a member of the Pakistani Parliament. Here she describes how she observed purdah starting at age nine, which for some upper class, strict families was considered to be late.

"This formal stepping into purdah made very little difference in my life. I did not go out of the house anyway, so all that it meant was that I did not now appear before the menservants and did not go to that part of the house where my father received his friends and that I now watched functions held there through chiks; these are pieces of bamboo curtain which are put up for ladies to see through without being seen. Ladies also watch through Venetian blinds. There is an art in opening it at the right angle so that one can see but not be seen. I never got the knack. According to my mother it was because I had been put in purdah too late. She said I never really learnt the art of living in purdah properly, and it is a fact that it is an art and it consists of many things besides knowing how to look without being seen yourself."[4]

1. Old "Pashto" saying (area of Northwestern India-Afghanistan).
2. Hanna Papenek, "Purdah: Separate Worlds and Symbolic Shelter," *Comparative Studies in Society and History.* Vol. 15, No. 3 (June, 1973), p. 289.
3. There are many variations of the purdah system in different parts of India and within different families.
4. Shaista S. Ikramullah, *From Purdah to Parliament* (London: The Cresset Press, 1963), p. 39.

A young Muslim married woman wears the burka she received at her wedding

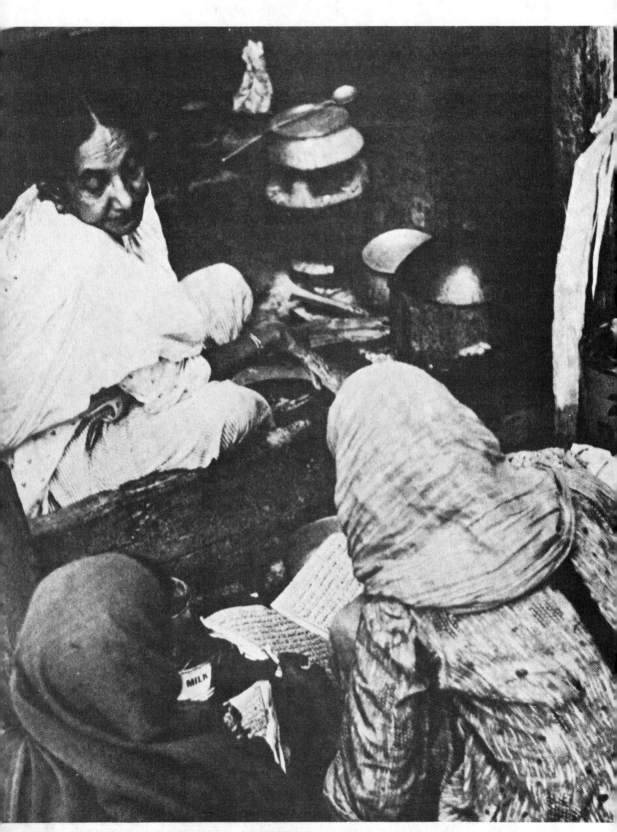

50   **Practice in Koran reading combined with household duties**

The "many things" that Begum Ikramullah refers to might be: learning not to look directly at people, wearing special coverings outside the home and anticipating the arrival of men into the home so women can go to their own quarters. These women's quarters, or zenanas, are described in a book by a Pakistani man, Mazhar Ul Hag Khan, called *Purdah and Polygamy*. He tells about three types of Muslim homes in India. Khan criticizes purdah and blames many problems of modern Pakistan on the purdah system.

"*There are* old-fashioned zenanas *[women's quarters] among the conservative and traditionalist sections and areas, in Pakistan especially in the backward, provincial towns and cities, where female seclusion is still a status symbol.... The architectural design of these zenanas varies from country to country, and even from city to city. These zenanas are houses in themselves as they are meant only for the females and children of the family. Men and grown-up boys of the family live mostly in a separate but adjacent building, usually called the "Mardana," the male guest house, which is either shared with other related families or owned by one individual family. The zenana house is built around a central courtyard or "sahn" with rooms or suite for several female inmates, especially as the master of the house may be polygynous [a man with more than one wife] and require accommodation for his several wives, their children and dependents. In the cities or towns, where living space is limited, the zenana portion is sometimes located in the* upper story *of the* house, *with the ground floor used for male quarters. A typical old-fashioned zenana is described by a woman novelist thus:*

'It consisted of a square courtyard surrounded by eight rooms, two on each side with a bathroom. All these rooms received light through a ventilator or a glass-tile in their ceiling. The only window that each room had opened on the courtyard and so also the doors.'

"*Another type of the zenanas is found in the* modern bungalow-like purdah houses. *The zenana in them is located in the rear portion of the house. It has a three-wall enclosure as its courtyard or sahn for the female inmates. The front portion of the house is used as the mardana or male quarters. There is no partition or purdah wall between the female and male portions of the house. Moreover, this type of zenana is, comparatively, more airy, brighter and cleaner.... This type, therefore, indicates modernistic trends in our Pakistani society.*

"*Finally,* non-purdah houses *are also coming into being, especially in fast developing modern cities and satellite towns, where zenanas as such may not exist. But even in such houses, the social atmosphere is purdah-like, because of the purdah environment around them. Nevertheless, the existence of such modern, non-purdah houses indicates the modernist trends in the Muslim society, which show that purdah is vanishing. The same trend is noticeable about the burka or chaddar,[5] the use of which is also decreasing among modernist sections.*

"*Besides these physical devices, purdah also implies the social customs, traditions and conventions, which exclude women from male company both inside the house as well as outside.... There are really two kinds of purdahs, namely, the outdoor purdah and the indoor purdah. The outdoor purdah is imposed on a girl as soon as she reaches the age of puberty, even earlier, especially in families and groups among whom it is strictly observed.*

5. heavy covering worn by women outside.

Roof terraces: women's domain

"Equally interesting, even more so, is the purdah inside the house, which divides the zenana from the mardana [male] portions of the house, but also imposes restrictions on free meetings and gatherings among family members, and other relatives -- though even here great variations are arising in the present times in different sections and areas of the Muslim society. However, these indoor restrictions prohibit admittance of even close male relatives into the zenana, such as uncles, cousins, even grown-up brothers and sons.

"The social atmosphere in the purdah families is full of restrictions, prohibitions, and fears. They start imposing purdah restrictions on little girls when they have hardly reached the age of eight or ten, and sometimes earlier.... So the purdah-born girl sees very little of her father and grown up brothers and still less of her grown up male cousins and relatives, even though they may be the members of her joint family or are occasional visitors. She grows up only in the company of the female inmates of the zenana.

"Purdah system thus plays a strangely divisive [dividing] role in the Muslim family and society. It not only excludes women from the outside world, it also excludes men from the inside world of the zenana, even though they are the most intimate members of the family, such as the husbands, fathers, or brothers. The father/husband spends most of his time outside in various activities. He has little or nothing to do with the "womanly" activities in the zenana except to take meals, which are often taken outside in the male or mardana quarters of the house along with other male members and visitors. Even when the father takes his meals in the zenana, he as well as other adult males, sits apart from the women and children. In the purdah families, the two sexes cannot even dine together. Even on such occasions as illness or death of a close relative in the male portion of the house, women are not allowed to attend or see him there."[6]

You have just read about Muslim purdahs. However, most Hindus also practiced a system of purdah. Historians disagree about the period when the purdah system began among Indian Hindus. Some trace the "guarding" and segregating of women back to the laws of Manu. Other historians blame the series of Muslim invasions for Hindu purdah. They say that Hindus copied the Muslim custom and, also, that women were put in purdah to protect them from these invaders. No matter which historical argument is correct, purdah was, and still is, practiced by many Indian Hindus. The following is a description of Hindu purdah.

Rama Mehta, an Indian social scientist, studied a group of Hindu women, the Oswals, in the city of Udaipur in Northwestern India. These women kept the strictest purdah long after most Hindus had given up many aspects of it. In the following selection Rama Mehta describes what that system required of Oswal women.

"Their houses reflected the pattern of life which they led; separated in the same house were the living quarters of men and women which ensured strict and guarded privacy. Women conducted their lives in their zenana. They were forbidden to enter the men's section even in their own house. In observing this pattern, the upper and lower classes adjusted their lifestyles according to their own means. Inside the city walls of Udaipur the big and small houses stand, all of them practically windowless, with courtyards that acted as barriers for segregation.

---

6. Mazhar Ul Hag Khan, *Purdah and Polygamy* (Peshawar: Nashiran e Iluo Taraqiyet, 1972), pp. 67-72.

Women wearing burkas to keep purdah outside their homes

"The Oswal girl from the age of seven was cautioned against playing outside; she was to stay within the zenana and amuse herself with other girls of her age, often of the maids.[7]

"During her childhood itself, she was carefully nurtured, trained into the discipline that she would have to observe in her adult life.... No one who had enjoyed unlimited freedom even as a child could later accept confinement within the walls of the zenana. The girl was imperceptibly [slowly] instructed in her obligations and duties and this training required time and tutoring....

"Purdah in the Oswal community was not only a means to segregate women from men but there was elaborate formality that governed the inter-personal relationship amongst women themselves. It prescribed that women should keep their faces covered from elder women of the family and of the community; it laid down with whom she could talk directly and with whom through an intermediary. The young Oswal bride very soon realised that in order to gain respect and status in the family, she had to be as invisible as possible and yet as useful as possible. There was a hierarchy [order of importance] of relatives, at the apex [top] of which was the mother-in-law; daughter-in-law stood at the lowest rung of the ladder. A daughter-in-law was never to talk to her mother-in-law directly, but only through either daughters of the house or maid-servants. This distance helped to keep authority undisputed and avert friction between generations.

The subordinate [lower] role of the daughter-in-law remained even after the active participation of the elders in the family had ceased. In talking to the majority of the older women (age group 65 to 80), I met women who had not seen the faces of their daughters-in-law even though they had lived in the same house for 20 to 30 years. Irrespective of the age of

the daughter-in-law, her face was always covered by a veil in front of elder female relatives."[8]

Mehta goes on to explain that, even though these women's lives were physically very restricted, they still were able to make contributions to the welfare of the community. They helped the poor, widows, and disabled people by gifts of food and money. They arranged marriages and were active in the affairs of their families. These women "did not while away their time in meaningless activity." However, in everything they did, they were dependent on men or servants. So, although they were "little queens" in their own windowless homes, they were absolutely restricted in the physical activities.

7. Servants, especially maids, were indispensible to a strict purdah system -- since purdah women rarely went outside and then were required to be completely covered and escorted.

8. Rama Mehta, "From Purdah to Modernity," in *Indian Women*, ed. B. R. Nanda (New Delhi: Vikas Publishing House, 1976), pp. 115-117.

A high caste Hindu woman with her face veiled

Points To Consider

1. Khan describes three types of zenanas. Which does he see as the most restrictive for women? Why?

   Even the "non-purdah" house is affected by the purdah system. In what ways?

2. Some of the earliest criticisms of the purdah system were that the zenanas were unhealthy places to live.
   A. Who lived in zenanas?
   B. What specific physical features of the zenanas possibly made them unhealthy places to live?

3. In what specific ways did the physical make up of the purdah home divide family members and friends? How do you think this would effect the emotional attachments between the following members:

   wife-husband
   mother-daughter
   mother-son
   father-daughter

4. Consider yourself to be a woman in purdah. Compare *one day* in your regular life to a day as a purdah woman. List those things that you would not be able to do.

5. Reformers who tried to change purdah were men. Why might it be *men* who tried to get rid of the purdah?

Chapter 4
Diversity of Roles

Chapter Contents

A. Tribal Women in India

Problems have been discussed that affect many women in historic or contemporary India: early marriage, the status of widows, sati, infanticide, and the purdah system. However, India is a vast area which is comprised of many groups of people. Women within different groups and in different periods of time have not followed the patterns of behavior described in Chapter III. Chapter IV will deal with the *exceptions* or *diverse*[1] roles of Indian women both past and present.

There are about 30 million "tribal" people living in modern India. The ancestors of these tribal groups were probably the original people of India when the Aryans invaded. Although many of them are Hindus, they have tended to keep many local customs which are different from those of the majority of Indian Hindus. The next selection is about one tribal group who evolved an interesting solution to the question of feminine "purity" and child marriage.

"Several aboriginal tribes and Hindu castes in the highlands of Chhattisgarh (Chh-ah-ttees-gar) close to the border of Madhya Pradesh and Orissa practice a form of token pre–puberty marriage which is in the nature of a rite de passage[2] for girls. This token marriage is known as kanda bara (arrow marriage) and appears to be a distinctive feature of this area. It is not confined to any particular ethnic group but is practised among communities of different economic and cultural levels.... In Chhattisgarh it is practised by a limited number of Hindu castes...

"Among all the Oriya-speaking castes of Western Orissa, with the exception of the Brahmans, a girl is married to an arrow before she reaches puberty, her actual marriage taking place much later.

"These tribes and castes have their own myths and legends to explain the origin and significance of this rite. The tribes trace its beginning to some of their legendary heroes who had a hand not only in the founding of the tribe but also in prescribing its distinctive way of life. The attitude of the Hindu castes on the other hand is that the custom originated from the decree of the Hindu gods and they seek to rationalize it on grounds of its practical utility.

"While the actual pattern of beliefs and rites connected with this ceremony differs from community to community, in broad outline they are similar. There is a general belief that until this ceremony is performed, the body of the girl remains 'unripe' and 'sacred.' Any sexual act or serious lapse on the part of the girl during this stage of her life would permanently defile her [make her impure or polluted]. Commencement of menstruation while she is in this state would similarly have an injurious effect on her body and would expose her parents to serious social disapproval and impair her own prestige in the community. Should this happen, she would have to suffer

1. Wide variety
2. Ceremonies for girls entering adulthood

The marriage to an arrow -- "groom" walks in front of the bride

certain social disabilities for the rest of her life. Important among these disabilities are the following:

1. She would not be able to marry according to full rites and ceremonies prescribed by tradition....

2. Because of her state of permanent pollution she would not be allowed to participate in any worship organized either by her family or the local group....

3. When a regular marriage ceremony is being performed she should not get too near the place where the bride and groom are seated, for both her touch and her shadow are believed to be impure and signify ill luck for the couple....

4. In general, too, a social stigma remains attached to her. First, any suspicion of witchcraft invariably falls on such a woman. People setting out to hunt, to negotiate a marriage, or on other important business seek to avoid her. For if they were to see her their pursuit would be followed by obstructions and difficulties, if not failure....

Tribal woman from Madhya Pradesh

"Among all the tribes and castes that practice this token marriage, child marriage is rare and adult marriage the general rule. The token pre-puberty marriage is a necessary preliminary preceding regular marriage and not a substitute for it. Most girls are married after puberty. But as they begin 'to understand the ways of the world' long before they approach the age of puberty, there is always some risk of their committing a sexual offence, and the menstruation of an 'unmarried' girl is regarded as highly undesirable. To protect her from any such danger, which would not only lower her social prestige and affect her life adversely, but would also bring disrepute to her family, recourse is taken to a token marriage. At the age of nine or ten the girl must be married in a token way to a prescribed object. Among the Chinda and the Chaukhutia Bhunjia she is married to an arrow. Among the Oriya-speaking Raj Gond this object is the branch of the mohua tree. Among the Hindu castes a girl is invariably married to a wooden pounder used for husking paddy. This token pre-puberty marriage is also known as 'the first marriage.' Once this ceremony is performed, the girl's body does not remain 'unripe' and 'sacred.' Now her offences and lapses may be treated by the tribal or caste authorities as are those of a married woman.

"The token pre-puberty marriage ceremony resembles a regular wedding in nearly all respects, except that it includes no engagement ceremony nor are any wedding gifts offered. The ceremony lasts two days, during which a [shortened] form of all the main rites of a regular marriage is performed.

"The applying of oil and tumeric to the bride and the token bridegroom, the taking-out of the marriage procession, the throwing of yellow rice, the going round the marriage post, and finally the ceremonial bathing of the bridal couple are all gone through step by step. A real brother-in-law (sister's husband) of the girl holds the token bridegroom in his hand and acts at the different stages of the ceremony on its behalf. For this service he receives a special gift of money or cloth at the time of the girl's regular marriage.

"It is well known that Manu, the supreme lawgiver of the Hindus, whose code still governs the fundamental structure of Hindu society, said that a girl should be married before the commencement of her menstruation, and child marriage has long been a feature of Hindu socio-religious life. But in tribal India, with a few exceptions, adult marriage coupled with considerable liberty during adolescence and early youth has been the general rule. The token pre-puberty marriage of the girls....[is a way that tribal people keep their girls "pure" while allowing them to marry later]. The Nayars of Travancore practice a similar ceremony before the girls reach the age of eleven 'to avoid reproach from friends and neighbors.' The Mysore Census Report of 1910 points out the existence of a [similar] custom among the Dhobis (washermen) of Mysore among whom post-puberty marriage is not debarred provided they have first been married to a tree or a sword."[3]

Points To Consider

1. Why did tribal people in the article marry their daughters to objects such as arrows, tree branches, or wooden pounders?

2. What useful purpose did these pre-puberty marriages have for these tribal people?

3. How did non-tribal Hindu society make sure their girls were "pure" upon marriage?

3. Dube, S.C., "Token Pre-Puberty Marriage in Middle India," *Man, Journal of the Royal Anthropological Institute*, Vol. 84, Nos. 24-25; February, 1953, pp. 1819.

B. Women in the Military: The Third Sex

"She was -- an influential and dangerous adversary"

In Stanley Wolpert's book on India, he discusses a group of women as part of a "Third Sex." For these women their *status* in society is so high that it overcomes their *role* as women. It may be individual wealth that sets the woman apart, or it may be family reputation. For example, Indira Gandhi was elected president of the Congress Party of India, filling the same role as her father Jawaharlal Nehru (jew-*ah*-herl-lahl *ney*-ru) and her grandfather Motilal Nehru (mo-*tee*-lahl *ney*-ru).

Women with high status even fulfilled the rather unlikely role as military leader. In a culture which stresses status obtained by being the *mother* of sons, it seems unlikely that they would be the *killer* of sons. However, some of the most famous stories of India are those in which the wife of a leader goes into battle to find or rescue her husband. Promila, for example, defeated an army and brought her husband back. The pantheon of Hindu gods also contains *Durga* who rides into battle on a lion. The Rajput of the Rajasthan area was particularly known for the princesses who received some military training.

In the nineteenth century, the British, who had not had a great female general since the days of Boudicca who fought against the Romans, were somewhat shocked to find themselves faced by armies led by women. The Great Mutiny or Sepoy Rebellion -- or as the Indians prefer to call it, the 1857 War of Independence -- saw several separate states trying to prevent their takeover by the British. The states of Jhansi, Ranearhand, and Oudh were controlled by women rulers, usually ruling until their sons came of age.

While several women were involved in military decisions, the woman who gave the British the most trouble was Rani Lakshmi Bai of Jhansi.

She was leader of the state of Jhansi when the British made plans to annex it and other Indian states to their empire. Refusing the cash settlement and pension offered to her by the British, she seems to have stayed out of the Mutiny of 1857 for a while. But historians suggest she probably aided the rebels with guns. When European civilians were massacred, British troops stepped up their attempt to control Jhansi. Rani Lakshmi Bai then fortified Jhansi and a siege began against British forces. Even British observers noticed her presence as a rallying point.

"It was sure," writes Malleson, *"that the Rani had infused some of her lofty spirit into her compatriots. Women and children were seen assisting in repair of the havoc made in the defense by the fire of besiegers and in carrying food and water to the soldiers on duty."*[1]

1. G.W. Malleson, *The Indian Mutiny, 1857-1859,* (London, 1906, Ninth edition), pp. 387-388.

63

"Promila"

After two months of fighting there was little left of the fortress and she and her son escaped. She then raised rebel forces and practiced guerrilla warfare. Planning a surprise attack, she and her troops captured the city of Gwaliar. Reinforced, the British returned to take the city. As she mounted her horse to escape, she was surrounded and shot. She died on the battlefield shortly after. Later Indian historians see her as a real patriot who lived and died for her country. The British historians who investigated the "mutiny" saw her as "an influential and dangerous adversary."[2]

It was the example of women like Rani Lakshmi Bai who also set a pattern for later women in their opposition to the British in the twentieth century. However, those imprisoned by rebellion in the twentieth century, like Vijaya Pandit (Vi-ji-ha *Pun*-det) or Sarojini Naidu, were more guided by Gandhian principles of non-violence than by Rajput military ideals. Some have suggested, though, that Indira Gandhi is not only a good example of the "Third Sex" because of her family background, but also because of her insistence on the role of the military in the India-China border war and domestic politics.

2. *Ibid.*, p. 221.

Indira Gandhi and Jawaharlal Nehru: Two Generations of Indian Prime Ministers

Points To Consider

1. What qualities might set certain women aside as members of a "Third Sex"?

2. Sometimes in history, as in the case of Joan of Arc, men have chosen to have a woman as their military leader. Why might having a woman leader be an asset? (Consider rival male factions, image of leader, the psychological effect on your enemy, etc.)

3. Looking at the number of women in the U.S. who have become governors or senators without their husbands holding the office before them, what would you say about the relevance of the "Third Sex" concept to the U.S. as well as India?

C. Women in Various Religious Roles

Prince Siddhartha Gautama, who became "The Buddha," was raised by his aunt, Queen Mahapajapati, because his mother died when he was an infant. After the death of her husband, Queen Mahapajapati led a group of widows to "The Buddha" to beg him to allow them to renounce the world and start an order of nuns. Twice he refused her request and only reluctantly agreed after his faithful follower, Ananda, spoke in favor of women.

Even though Buddhist nuns were held to stricter standards of behavior than Buddhist monks, many women joined Buddhist orders, and became Buddhist preachers or poets. The following fragments of poems were written by early Buddhist nuns.

Lo: from my heart the hidden shaft
is gone.
The shaft that nestled there she
hath removed.
And that consuming grief for my
dead child,
Which poisoned all the life of me,
is dead.
Today my heart is healed, my
yearning stayed.
Perfected the deliverance wrought
in me.
Lo: I for refuge to the Buddha
go --
The only wise -- The Order and the
Norm.

O woman well set free: How free
am I
How thoroughly free from kitchen
drudgery.

O free indeed: O glorious free
Am I in freedom from three crooked
things --
From quern,[1] from mortar, from my
crookbacked lord;
Ay, but I'm free from rebirth and
from death,
And all that dragged me back is
hurled away.[2]

Hinduism has several cults that emphasize the importance of women. These groups worship the "female principle" or creative part of the universe -- in the form of woman and mother. They are called Shakti (wife of Shiva, female energy) or Tantric Cults. For believers in "Shakti" or "Tantric," liberation and spirituality are not found by giving up worldly pleasures (as in Buddhism and some other Hindu cults) but by enjoying the good things of life. Their main female God, Shakti, is superior to her

1. A quern is a grinding tool for grains.
2. Quoted in: Padmini Sengupta, *Women in India* (New Delhi: Information Service of India, 1974), pp. 75-76.

Holy woman staring at the sun

husband, Shiva. She is the female God of beauty, riches, and desire. But there are as many as one thousand Tantric female Gods. Some of them are fierce and ugly, some calm and beautiful -- all represent a different aspect of part of Shakti, their supreme female God.

BHAKTI - Women As Mystics

Another example of a Hindu cult that appealed to women was the Bhakti Cult. It became popular in the twelfth century A.D. because it promised its followers salvation (or heaven) if they were completely devoted to God. After the Vedic Age, women were no longer allowed to say the Vedas and make Vedic sacrifices. Thus, women could only attain heaven through their husband by being completely devoted to him. In fact, Hinduism classified women with Sudras -- as having such low status that they were not even allowed to study the Vedas. The new Bhakti Cult of Hinduism said that anyone could attain salvation who showed complete devotion and love to God. This sect appealed to both women and to low caste men. Several female Bhakti followers became saints and poets. Their poem-hymns are still popular in India today.

Points To Consider

1. List several specific reasons why some women might want to become Buddhist nuns.

2. What might the Shakti and Bhakti sects have to offer women that orthodox Hinduism might not have offered?

D. The Devadasi

"Single Woman as the Common Woman"

Indian culture did not have a respectable place or role for single adults. All people were expected to marry. Finding a marriage partner was more difficult for the parents of girls: they had to find a man of the proper caste, provide a dowry, a wedding, and give their daughter away as a gift to strangers. What did a family do that had many daughters and little money? One solution was to dedicate or "marry" a daughter to God as a *Devadasi.*

The custom of dedicating girls to temples to be married to the God probably dates from c. 300 A.D., but became common by the eleventh century A.D. Devadasi means "slave of God." Parents gave their daughter to a temple as an offering to the God.[1]

In early times these girls were well educated. They could dance, sing, and play musical instruments. They enjoyed high social status. By 1000 A.D., however, their role had degenerated to that of "temple prostitute." Even though their social standing was low, prostitutes in India are considered to be "good luck" -- unlike widows who were considered to be bad luck.

Recently a sociological study was done of prostitution in the Indian city of Bombay. One third of the women prostitutes interviewed had been given to the temples as Devadasi even though it is now against Indian law to dedicate girls to temples. Most of these Devadasi came from rural areas and one half of them were "harijans" (untouchables).[2] Indian reformers, such as Gandhi and Reddi,[3] realized that this Devadasi system exploited (used) the poorest and lowest caste girls. These reformers worked hard to get temple prostitution outlawed. Although the custom of Devadasis continues to be a problem in India, reformers hope the changes in the law will eventually eliminate the custom of "temple prostitution."

Point to Consider

List several reasons why you think that temple prostitution has continued in India even though it is against the law.

1. Eventually girls were also dedicated to female gods -- Devadasi having lost the idea of marriage.
2. S.D. Punekar and Kamala Rao, *A Study of Prostitutes in Bombay* (Bombay: Lalvani Publishing House, 1967), pp. 178-189.
3. These reformers are discussed in a later section of the book.

Nautch girls or dancing girls -- similar to Devadasi

E. Low Caste and High Caste Women

After studying the information below each continuum, decide where low caste women fall on each continuum compared to high and middle caste women. (Use H=High Caste, M=Middle Caste, L=Low Caste)

In what areas do low caste women have more options than high and middle caste women? What groups of women seem to have the most restricted lives?

AGE OF MARRIAGE

age 5-12	12-15	16-20	above 20

HIGH CASTES

Differ greatly: for example, some still approve of early marriage (Rajputs of a central Indian village prefer girls to be married before 12.)[1] Brahmans especially seem to prefer early marriages.

Some urban and village high castes, who emphasize education as a desirable addition to a girl's "dowry," desire later marriages.[2]

MIDDLE CASTES

Same as high castes: probably are moving toward more education for girls, so a higher marriage age; however, village middle castes still marry their girls between 14-16.

LOW CASTES

Still prefer early marriages, probably below legal limit of 15 for girls.[3]

PURDAH AND PHYSICAL FREEDOM

Purdah (separate living quarters for men and women; veiling of women)	**Some veiling** (veiling depends upon family relations)	**"Western"** (no separation of men and women at home; no veiling; physically quite independent)

1. Bhagvant Rao Dubey, "Widow Remarriage in Madhya Pradesh," *Man in India*, Vol. 45, 1, March, 1965, p. 51.
2. Mildred Stroop Luschinsky, "The Impact of Some Recent Indian Government Legislation on the Women of an Indian Village," *Asian Survey*, Vol. 3, No. 12, p. 578.
3. *Ibid.*, p.578

HIGH CASTES

Brahmans and Kshatriya seem to have been the first groups to encourage a strict purdah system among females. Some of these castes still maintain strict purdah for women.

High caste, educated, city women have completely given up purdah and work as professionals outside the home.

MIDDLE CASTES

Those castes or sub-castes which have a desire to better themselves in the caste hierarchy, who want to move up in status, tend to copy the high castes.[4] These castes/sub-castes tend to keep the strictest purdah systems. For example, their women quit their outside jobs, stay at home, and are secluded by purdah.

Among a second group of middle castes, for example some agriculturalists, strict purdah is not kept because the women work in the fields, houses are small, etc. These women would observe "respectful" veiling at home -- for example a young bride would cover her face in front of her father-in-law, older brothers of her husband, etc.

LOW CASTES

Everyone works, therefore, strict purdah is impossible. Huts are too small for separate quarters. There is some "respectful" covering of women's faces at home.

WIDOW REMARRIAGE AND DIVORCE

Not allowed	Disapproved of but sometimes occurs	Encouraged/allowed

HIGH CASTES

Rajputs (Kshatriya) and Brahmans still do not "allow" widow remarriage. Remarriage would probably mean being put out of the caste and completely condemned by an individual's caste community. They were the only groups to practice sati (first Kshatriya and later the Brahmans) until about 1400 A.D. These groups strongly disapprove of divorce -- almost unheard of among them except in certain areas of India.

MIDDLE CASTES

Widows can remarry, but only to widowers. Among agriculturalists, women (wives) are badly needed for their labor because they work both in the home and in the fields. Also, because they are so valuable, a widow's father often receives a "bride price," therefore, economic and social pressures encourage widow remarriage.[5] Divorce is frowned on. Sati is practiced occasionally after c. 1400 or 1500 A.D.

LOW CASTES

Always allowed remarriage of widows. Also, by custom these castes allowed divorce and remarriage even when it was "unheard of" in other castes.[6]

4. This is called "Sanskritisation" by Indian social scientists. It means the copying of members of a higher caste by a lower caste or sub-caste to gain status for the lower caste group.
5. Dubey, "Widow Remarriage," pp. 50-55.
6. Luschinsky, "Impact," p. 573.

Chapter 5

Nineteenth and Twentieth Century Reform

Chapter Contents

In the nineteenth and twentieth centuries, India -- like many other countries -- went through a series of reform movements. India's, however, were complicated by the complexities of its caste system, the diversity of its geographical areas, and by the presence of the **British**. When it came to reform concerning women, the picture was further complicated by what the British might see as a "lady" or what the Indian saw as the role for women. A British woman traveling in India was horrified to see Indian women raise their dresses to cover their faces. She saw them as immodest creatures showing their ankles, even their knees! They were, in Indian eyes, very modestly maintaining their privacy of face.

But despite cultural differences, both Indian and British reformers acted to change views toward women. One of the most famous of the Indian reformers was Rammohun Roy who worked hard for education of women and better conditions for widows especially. The organization he founded, Brahmo Samaj, tried to incorporate Western reform ideas to change Hindu beliefs. Another group, Arya Samaj, founded by Dayanand Saraswati, did not wish to emphasize Western influences, but went back to Vedic texts to show the change that had occurred over the centuries. They pointed out that in Vedic times women could choose their own partners (Swayambara), that they moved freely without purdah, and that child marriages were not the case. Later Indian reformers noted for supporting the improvement in the status of women included men like Madadev Coovinda Ranade (*Ran*-ah-day), Mahatma Gandhi, and Jawaharlal Nehru, and women like Cornelia Sorojini, Muthulaskshmi Reddi, and Pandita Ramabai. (*Ram*-ah-bye)

British and American missionaries and government officials also became involved in women's roles in India. American funds helped Pandita Ramabai's first home for widows.

The Salvation Army set up girls' schools, especially for untouchable, low caste girls. William Bentinck, a British governor, outlawed sati.

British women, like Annie Besant and Margaret Cousins, worked in movements to help Indian women gain political and economic rights.

Sometimes the foreign attempts at reform seemed somewhat misguided. One school had young girls specializing in fine needlework, more suitable for Victorian lace doilies, when their simple homes would not have tables and chairs.

Also, sometimes homes for widows were criticized by such nationalist leaders as Tilak for trying to convert women to Christianity rather than trying to help them function in their own society.

The reform concerning women in India was one filled with problems. It was also one in which many took part; men and women of a variety of backgrounds -- from an Irish revolutionary woman to a high caste Brahman man, from a British governor to a woman Parsi lawyer, from a man revered as "Mahat" to a woman who had lost her parents in starvation.

To show what these reformers faced, the following selections represent three specific areas of Indian reform -- sati, widow remarriage, and the education of women.

**William Bentinck, British
Governor – against Sati**

**Raja Rammohun Roy,
Indian Reformer**

A. Westerners' Views of Sati

When various travelers came into India, one of the most startling customs of India they saw was sati, the burning of widows. There are hardly any travel accounts that do not mention some confrontation with this custom. The reactions of the visitors varied, however. When Ibn Battuta saw his first sati, he found himself feeling faint and almost fell off his horse; he then rode away. His view was that in the future he would avoid all of the barbarous customs of the infidel Indians. The Muslim ruler, Akbar, did try to outlaw sati, but without much success. The French traveler, Francois Bernier, was so indignant at seeing a sati, that he rescued the woman and promised a pension to the family as long as the woman was allowed to live. Other travelers describe rescue attempts in which the rescuers had to fight off the villagers who were trying to drag the widow back into the fire. Some travelers simply mention with admiration the courage of the widows as they accepted their fate and the fire. Other travelers saw women being pushed into the flames or mentioned the untouchable caste of men who showed up at funerals. Their hope was for a young, beautiful widow to lose courage and then they might claim her, as she would no longer have any respect from her family.

The British East India Company generally took the view that less trouble would be caused in trade if they just left Indian customs alone. However, some of the later British officials felt that in all conscience they could not allow widow burnings. William Bentinck, British governor in the early nineteenth century, outlawed them in British controlled areas in 1840.[1]

There were, however, some who felt they did not have the right to interfere with another country's value system. The following is an excerpt from the journal of William Sleeman, a British official in India in the 1830's, describing his conversation with a widow:

"On Tuesday, 24th November, 1829, I had an application from the heads of the most respectable and most extensive family of Brahmans in the district to suffer this old woman to burn herself with the remains of her husband, who had that morning died upon the banks of the Nerbudda.[2] I threatened to enforce my order and punish severely any man who assisted; and placed a police guard for the purpose of seeing that no one did so. She remained sitting by the

1. Sati was outlawed in Bengal in 1829, but not in other areas until 1840.
2. Whenever it is practicable, Hindus are placed on the banks of sacred rivers to die, especially in Bengal.

76

edge of the water without eating or drinking. The next day the body of her husband was burned to ashes in a small pit .... before several thousand spectators who had assembled to see the suttee. All strangers dispersed before evening, as there seemed to be no prospect of my yielding to the urgent solicitations of her family, who dared not touch food till she had burned herself, or declared herself willing to return to them. Her sons, grandsons, and some other relations remained with her, while the rest surrounded my house, the one urging me to allow her to burn, and the other urging her to desist.

"She remained sitting on a bare rock in the bed of the Nerudda, refusing every kind of food, and exposed to the intense heat of the sun by day, and the severe cold of the night, with only a thin sheet thrown over her shoulders.

"On Thursday, to cut off all hope of her being moved from her purpose, she put on the dhaja, or coarse red turban, and broke her bracelets in pieces, by which she became dead in law, and forever excluded from caste. Should she choose to live after this, she could never return to her family. Her children and grandchildren were still with her, but all their entreaties were unavailing; and I became satisfied that she would starve herself to death, if not allowed to burn, by which the family would be disgraced, her miseries prolonged, and I myself rendered liable to be charged with abuse of authority [for the British government had not yet outlawed sati].[3]

"On Saturday, the 28th, in the morning, I rode out ten miles to the spot, and found the poor old widow sitting with the dhaja round her head, a brass plate before her with undressed rice and flowers, and a coconut in each hand. She talked very collectedly, telling me that 'she had determined to mix her ashes with those of her departed husband,

and should patiently wait my permission to do so, assured that God would enable her to sustain life till that was given, though she dared not eat or drink.' Looking at the sun, then rising before her over a long and beautiful reach of the Nerbudda river, she said calmly, 'My soul has been for five days with my husband's near that sun, nothing but my earthly frame is left; and this, I know, you will in time suffer to be mixed with the ashes of his in yonder pit, because it is not in your nature to prolong the miseries of a poor old woman.'

"'Indeed, it is not -- my object and duty is to save and preserve them; and I am come to dissuade you from this idle purpose, to urge you to live, and to keep your family from the disgrace of being thought your murderers.'

"'I am not afraid of their ever being so thought: they have all, like good children, done everything in their power to induce me to live among them; and, if I had done so, I know they would have loved and honored me; but my duties to them have now ended. I commit them all to your care, and I go to attend my husband, Ummed Singh Upadhya.'

"This was the first time in her long life that she had ever pronounced the name of her husband, for in India no woman, high or low, ever pronounces the name of her husband.... When the old lady named her husband, as she did with strong emphasis, and in a very deliberate manner, every one present was satisfied that she had resolved to die.... 'My soul is with Ummed Singh Upadhya' she said, 'and my ashes must here mix with his.'

"Again looking to the sun -- 'I see them together,' said she, with a tone and countenance that affected me a

---

3. Sati was not outlawed by the British government until 1829 (Bengal), other areas in 1840.

good deal, 'under the bridal canopy!' -- alluding to the ceremonies of marriage; and I am satisfied that she at that moment really believed that she saw her own spirit and that of her husband under the bridal canopy in paradise.

"Satisfied myself that it would be unavailing to attempt to save her life, I sent for all the principal members of the family, and consented that she should be suffered to burn herself if they would enter into engagements that no other member of their family should ever do the same. This they all agreed to, and the papers having been drawn out in due form about midday, I sent down notice to the old lady, who seemed extremely pleased and thankful.

"The ceremonies of bathing were gone through before three [o'clock], while the wood and other combustible materials for a strong fire were collected and put into the pit. After bathing, she called for a 'pan' (betel leaf) and ate it, then rose up, and with one arm on the shoulder of her eldest son, and the other on that of her nephew, approached the fire. I had sentries placed all round, and no other person was allowed to approach within five paces. As she rose up fire was set to the pile, and it was instantly in a blaze. The distance was about 150 yards. She came on, calm and cheerful, stopped once, and casting her eyes upward, said, 'Why have they kept me five days from thee, my husband?' On coming to the sentries her supporters stopped; she walked once round the pit, paused a moment, and, while muttering a prayer, threw some flowers into the fire. She then walked up deliberately and steadily to the brink, stepped into the center of the flame, sat down, and leaning back in the midst as if reposing upon a couch, was consumed without uttering a shriek or betraying one sign of agony."[4]

4. W.H. Sleeman, *Rambles and Recollections of an Indian Official*, (Oxford University Press, 1915), pp. 18-23.

Points To Consider

Values Exercise:

1. After reading this selection, what would you have done in Sleeman's place?

2. What reasons do *you* see as being the most important for making your decision?

3. The following list contains commonly given reasons for British actions on the problem of sati. Which two do you see as the most acceptable reasons; which two do you see as being least acceptable. Explain your choices.

   1. Widow's life would be "cold sati" anyway, might as well end her misery fast.

   2. All human life has a value, should be preserved.

   3. The British are here for trade, why stir up trouble.

   4. Every nation is entitled to have its own customs, let the old woman die happy in fulfilling her "duty."

   5. Saving one widow will set an example for the rest of the culture to change, thereby saving their widows who might be unwilling.

   6. The "higher" races (i.e., British) have a duty to educate and civilize the "lesser" (i.e., Indian); so this barbarous custom should be stopped.

   7. The resources of India are so meager and poor, the society can't afford to keep dependent, old people.

   8. Do nothing to interfere; it's an Indian problem; they will eventually stop it themselves.

   9. The widow could be useful to her family and now her grandchildren will never know her.

   10. Who cares if Indians kill each other off, these people are not worth bothering with.

You have decided to stop sati; which of the following would you use as a *means* for doing so. Why?

1. Give pension plans for widows, set up homes for them.

2. Use force to stop burnings, arrest anyone who participates.

3. Go to the people to educate them to change.

4. Outlaw Hinduism as a religion.

5. Help organize Indian-led reform groups.

The Practice of Sati: An Activity to Interpret Sources

In the last exercise you may have noticed how difficult it often is for outsiders to evaluate or change a custom they are unfamiliar with. In the next exercise you will have a chance to read a number of different statements about the custom of sati or "widow burning."

Read through these sources. They represent descriptions of actual sources that appeared in print. Evaluate the sources below as indicated. Work in small groups or as individuals. Record your answers on a sheet of paper. Before you begin to decide how to classify each source, discuss the terms "primary" and "secondary" sources within your group.

Primary Sources:
Eye witness accounts of people who actually were involved in or saw the events described in writing or pictures. Primary sources have the advantage of the observer having immediate contact with the event. However, their reporting may be distorted by limitations of their points of view.

Secondary Sources:
Interpretations of events by people who did not witness them. They may be by scholars -- such as historians -- who collect a great deal of source material about an event.

Evaluate each of the following ten sources as follows:

Check One

_____ Primary Source
_____ Secondary Source
_____ Not Sure

Write a short explanation of why you selected "primary," "secondary" or "not sure" for each source.

1. *"...Nearly every year an illegal 'suttee' [Sati] comes before the courts...They would be of little importance if they did not obviously arouse great popular enthusiasm. The 1927 Sati was the heroine of the countryside, and vast crowds visited the place of her immolation...."* G.T. Garrat, *An Indian Commentary*, (Jonathan Cape, London, 1928), p. 235.[1]

2. *"...At Bahrol there is a very unusual number of tombs built over the ashes of women who have burnt themselves with the remains of their husbands....On one stone of this kind I saw...the figure of a horse in bas-relief, and I asked one of the gentlemen farmers, who was riding with me, what it meant. He told me that he thought it indicated that the woman rode on horseback to bathe before she ascended the pile." Major-General W.H. Sleeman,* Rambles and Recollections of an Indian Official (London: Humphrey Milford, 1915, new edition), p. 109.

1. Quoted in: Katherine Mayo, *Slaves of the Gods* (New York: Harcourt, Brace and Company, 1929).

3. *"The earliest historical instance of Sati is that of the wife of the Hindu general Keteus, who died in 316 B.C. while fighting against Antigonos. Both the wives of the general were very anxious to accompany their husband on the funeral pyre, but as the elder one was with child, the younger one alone was allowed to carry out her wish.* A.S. Altekar, *The Position of Women in Hindu Civilization* (Bauaras: Motilal, 1956), p. 122.

4. *"Monday 7th, I saw the dismal Spectacle of a wretched Pagan Woman...Burn'd with the dead Body, according to their wicked unmerciful Custom. In the Afternoon the Woman came out well Clad, and adorn'd with Jewels,...after which she was laid all along, with her Head on a Block, in a Cottage twelve Spans square, made of small Wood wet with Oil, but bound to a Stake, that she might not run away with the fright of the Fire. Lying in this Posture, chewing Betelle, she ask'd of the Standers by, whether they had any Business by her to the other World...the Brahman, who had been Encouraging of her, came out of the Hut, and caus'd it to be Fir'd; the Friends pouring Vessels of Oil on her, that she might be the sooner reduc'd to Ashes, and out of Pain."* John Careri, *A Voyage Around the World* (New Delhi: National Archives, 1949, new edition), p. 211-212.

5. *"A memorable act of Lord William Bentinck's government, and the one with which his name will be most prominently associated in history, was the abolition of Widow-burning...the abolition by a short resolution of a practice sanctioned by religion and the usage of centuries was more calculated to arrest public attention and to obtain general applause than measures passed from time to time at the Council board."* Demetrius Boulger, *Lord William Bentinck* (Oxford: Clarendon Press, 1892).

6. *"The extent to which Sati prevailed in Central India especially is brought home by the innumerable sati stones. There is considerable variety in the form these memorials take. Many are just upstanding stones marked with a woman's hand, often a vermilioned hand. The sati, setting out to die, marked the lintel of her home with her hand, freshly stained with the red stain that decks the bride.... Many of these hands still decorate houses."* Edward Thompson, *Suttee* (London: Allen and Unwin, 1928), p. 30.

7. *"...the fatal belief that a Sati's resolution once voluntarily taken is irrevocable, may have caused the bystanders to thrust the victim remorselessly back into the flames; or if, from British interposition, a rescue has been effected, the woman has, it may be, survived only to curse the pity which, to save her from a few moments of pain, has deprived her, as she deemed, of ages of happiness. These things have been; but, with rare exceptions, the Sati is a voluntary victim."* Henry Jeffreys Bushby, *Widow-Burning* (London: Longman, Brown, Green and Longman, 1855), p. 18.

8. *"In regard to the women who actually burn themselves, I was present at so many of those shocking exhibitions that I could not persuade myself to attend any more, nor is it without a feeling of horror that I revert to the subject. I shall endeavor, nevertheless, to describe what passed before my eyes;... When traveling from Ahmed-abad to Agra...news reached us that a widow was then on the point of burning herself with the body of her husband. I ran at once to the spot, and going to the edge of a large and nearly dry reservoir, observed at the bottom a deep pit filled with wood: the body of a dead man extended thereon; a woman seated upon the same pile; four or five Brahmans setting fire to it in every part; five middle-aged women, tolerably well dressed, holding one another by the hand, singing and dancing round the pit;*

and a great number of spectators of both sexes." Francois Bernier, *Travels in the Mogul Empire, 1656-1668* (Delhi: S. Chand and Co., 1968, modern edition), p. 309–310.

9. *"The practice of burning or burying women alive with their deceased husbands, even as an expression of an underlying view of women as property, is not as bizarre and exotic a custom as its identification with Hindu India has made it seem.... The practice apparently originated among warriors who probably also elaborated the mythology attached to it. The heroism of the Sati (the sacrificed woman) was in fact equated with that of the warrior. The connection of suttee with the warrior and ruler (Ksatriya) caste endowed it with a social prestige which it never lost."* Dorothy Stein, "Women to Burn," *Signs,* Vol. 4, No. 2 (Winter, 1978), p. 253.

10. ..."Once in the town of Amjari I *saw three women whose husbands had been killed in battle and who had agreed to burn themselves.... The fire was screened off by a blanket held by some men, so that [one of the women] should not be frightened by the sight of it. I saw one of them, on coming to the blanket, pull it violently out of the men's hands, saying to them with a smile, 'Do you frighten me with the fire? I know that it is a fire, so let me alone.' Thereupon she joined her hands above her head in salutation to the fire and cast herself into it."* Ibn Battuta, *Travels in Asia and Africa, 1325–1354* (London: George Routledge, 1929, modern edition), p. 192–193.

B. Widow Remarriage

In 1856 a law was passed that allowed Indian widows to remarry. However, by custom, it was still prohibited among high caste Indians. In the following account you will see that this prohibition against widow remarriage affected both women and men. A nineteenth century reformer and Brahman, D.K. Karve (*Kur*-vey), tells about his decision to marry a widow after the death of his first wife.

"Whenever I thought of marrying again, the prospect of marrying a girl who was young enough to be my daughter frightened me. There was no possibility of marrying anyone older, because no girl remained unmarried beyond the age of twelve or thirteen in those days. Naturally the question of marrying a widow came to my mind.[1] I had thought about this matter even when I was a boy. Widow remarriage was quite unknown among the higher castes although one or two such marriages had taken place. I was only eleven years old when the first such marriage was celebrated in Bombay in 1869... This event produced a great commotion in Maharashtra.[2] In 1871, a public discussion among learned Brahmans was held in Poona[3] to determine whether the marriage of widows had the sanction of the ancient Hindu lawbooks. The verdict was six to four against the marriage of widows, and the religious elder gave his final decision in accordance with that.

"Another event brought the matter again into my thoughts. A friend and fellow student of mine took the lead in arranging the marriage of his young widowed sister. As the event took place at Jabalpur, several

hundred miles from Poona and Bombay, it did not attract much attention, but it did leave an impression on my mind. A different kind of incident, which I remember very well, took place about the time when I appeared for the public service examination. An orthodox priest who lived not far from our house had a daughter whose husband had abandoned her. She was living in her father's house, wearing the red Kunku mark on her forehead,[4] when somehow she fell victim to some unscrupulous man. She continued to live in the family until her condition could no longer be concealed but had to leave the house after that. The father was threatened with excommunication by the village council for having harbored a sinner and had to pay a heavy penalty.

"Some years later I met the woman in a place of pilgrimage in southern Maharashtra which incurably sick people, women in difficulties, and lunatics often seek out. The poor creature saw me while she was going round and round the temple counting her rounds on the beads of a rosary and turned her face away. The episode left an indelible impression on my mind.

1. (The term "widow" here refers to a girl whose husband has died before the marriage was consummated.) Notice that Karve was talking about only widows whose marriages had not been "consummated" -- in other words, virgin child widows who had never lived with their husbands. We assume that even he would not have married a widow who had lived with her husband and, perhaps, had children by her first husband.
2. Maharashtra is a west-central state of modern India.
3. Poona is a large city in Maharashtra.
4. All women who are not widows wear the red Kunku mark on their foreheads in Maharashtra.

D. D. Karve, Indian reformer who married a widow

"Now after I had been in Poona for some time, not only friends but my brother and mother began to press me to give my consent to a second marriage. In those days marrying a widow meant being cut off from society, especially in the case of persons who had relatives living in the rural areas, which were very orthodox. My first task was, therefore, to persuade my brother and my mother. They were very good-natured and had a high regard for me. No doubt my marrying a widow would cause them great humiliation and they had to prepare themselves to face it. I also told them that if they did not give me their consent, I would prefer to remain a widower throughout my life. They were thus in a dilemma. They realised how strong my convictions were, but they also knew what they would have to endure in our village. Finally, however, they gave me permission to do what I thought right, provided however that I did not involve them in any way.

"The next question was perhaps more difficult in the society in which I was living, namely, to find a suitable bride. Some friends had actually suggested some suitable widows as possibilities, but I was hesitant and could not make up my mind. The question was solved in an unexpected manner. My friend Joshi had a younger sister named Godu, who had been widowed at the age of eight. She had lived in the family of her late husband until she was about twenty-three, when Joshi brought her to Bombay intending to educate her. She lived in our joint family for a few months before she was admitted to the famous Pandita Ramabai's [5] school as its first widow student. When the school later moved from Bombay to Poona, Godubai [6] went

5. This famous Sanskrit scholar and reformer was converted to Christianity in 1883. Her school is now being conducted under the auspices of the Church Missionary Society.
6. *bai* in Maharashtra is a word meaning woman, attached to proper names; it is also a term of address for married women in parts of North India.

with it. Her head had been shaved according to the prevalent custom, and as her parents were orthodox in their views, the idea of marrying her never entered my mind.

"About this time Joshi's father was in Poona on a short visit and came to see me. To my surprise he asked me directly why I had not married again. When I told him of my intention of marrying a widow if at all, he remained silent for a few minutes and then replied that, in that case, I did not have to go far to seek a suitable bride. I replied that I understood what he had in mind but asked whether he was serious. When he answered in the affirmative, I requested him to see his daughter to ask whether she was agreeable to the proposal.

"He [the elder Mr. Joshi] went to Godubai's school and reported to me that she was willing to marry me. I also learned that the head of the school had persuaded her not to submit to the barber and she had let her hair grow. She was thus ready to marry me as soon as convenient. Her father could not, of course, associate himself openly with the marriage and went away to his village.

"My friends were ready to help in all the arrangements. It was the first marriage of a widow to be celebrated in Poona, and they wanted to make it an important event. The question of a house in which to celebrate the wedding would normally have been difficult but a householder whose widowed daughter had herself been married in Bombay some years back came forward and offered his house. We even secured the services of a very learned priest with advanced views in this matter, although a couple of my friends were prepared to recite the sacred verses and perform the religious ceremonies if it became necessary.

"My second marriage was celebrated on March 11, 1893. It caused a great commotion all over Maharashtra. Personally it did not involve much change in my daily routine, but apart from newspaper comments, my brother and my mother had to bear a considerable amount of persecution and condemnation in our village."[7]

Points To Consider

1. What makes Karve decide to marry a widow after the death of his first wife?

2. How does he go about finding a new wife to marry? How does this contrast with a person remarrying in our culture?

7. D.D. Karve, The New Brahmans (Berkeley: University of California, 1963), pp. 39-42.

C. Education for Women

Women in various periods in Indian history had been educated. In Vedic times women were taught to say the Vedas, Buddhist nuns were learned and, in the twelfth century, the Bhakti Hindu sect encouraged women poets. The Muslim era had various women who were poets and started libraries. But the amount of education for women declined over the centuries, partly perhaps as child marriages at ages 5–9 meant that the girl's family saw no real reason to invest much education in her. The groom's family also seems not to have emphasized education. There were some exceptional families like the one Pandita Ramabai came from whose mother and father were both Vedic scholars and made her one also. But she was so unusual, even in late nineteenth century India, that she was specifically addressed with the title, Sarasvati, meaning "learned one."

But it was not just women's education that posed problems for nineteenth and twentieth century reformers. The issue of education was a disturbing one in India partly because reading and writing had been more of a caste role with the Brahmans being the most educated. Furthermore, as the British tried to help set up educational systems in India, they found a wide variety of languages. Unable to cope -- or unwilling to cope -- with such diversity of language, they made English the "national" language. When it came to education for women, they did set up colleges for women, but widespread basic education -- for boys as well as girls -- was not instituted. There were, however, particular problems in raising the literacy rates among women. The following list suggests some of these problems:

1. There were no respectable roles for single women -- so there were no single women available to be devoted school teachers as in the U.S. and England.

2. Male teachers would violate purdah restrictions. Parents often refused to send girls to schools with male teachers.

3. The poverty of the country was such that educational funds were limited and available funds often went to educate boys.

4. Women were thought to need no education since their role was seen as domestic and they could learn these skills at home.

Even with these difficulties Indian women, especially those in more well-to-do homes, were being educated. Often though, their education clashed with other values of the joint household and led to problems. Madadev Govinda Ranade was forced by his family into a second marriage with an eleven-year old girl. Since he was in his late 20's and interested in reform, he seems to have been rather embarrassed by suddenly having a child bride who could neither read nor write. In order that she might eventually become a real companion to him, he tried to start her early down a path different from the one followed by the rest of the women in the family. His encouragement and support helped her later to become one of India's better known reformers. But as she tells it, it was a rather painful path -- even with his support. The following selection tells of her attempts at learning to read and to speak English.

"I completed my Marathi lessons and my husband began to teach me English. Now it was not enough to do my lessons only at night and early in the morning. I had to sit an hour or more to learn the words by heart. There was no place to do that downstairs. I had to go upstairs to our room. That made the women all the more furious. Once they said to me, 'You may do what you like in your room. But we cannot tolerate disrespectful behavior.'

"One afternoon the women were all relaxing in the back verandah after the midday meal. I was sweeping the middle hall. In the midst of it, I came across a piece of English newspaper. In my youthful enthusiasm, I thought I had attained proficiency in what I had just begun to learn and that I would be able to read it. So I put down the broom and stood trying to read the piece of paper. I had opened the first reader only a fortnight before. How could I read! I just stood and gazed at the letters. I quite forgot that I was downstairs. At this moment, my grand-mother-in-law noticed me and signalled to the others near me. I was unconcerned. My sister-in-law was furious at this and shouted, 'Your hapees (office) is upstairs. There you may read or

Pandita Ramabai: Sanskrit Scholar and Educator

write. *But you shall not insult us!*
That late sister-in-law of ours could
read and write. She was of our age.
And yet she never indulged in reading
a single letter in our presence.'

"That was the kind of talk that went
on constantly. Often I greatly
regretted having started to learn
English. I was at my wits' end, and
when it became too much for me, I
would weep secretly to myself. But I
never said a word of this to my
husband. I remembered that when I
was first coming away to my father-
in-law's house, my father had drawn
me to himself and advised me.

"He had said, 'Listen girl, you are
going to your father-in-law's. It is a
family of many relations -- even
step-relations. There are many
dependents, too. You are my
daughter. Put up with everything
patiently, however unbearable it
might be; but never answer back --
not even servants.... If I ever learn
that you have behaved contrary to
this, I shall never bring you back to
your mother's home again.'

Further family eruptions occurred
after an English woman was brought
in to help with the teaching.

"The anger which had been
smouldering slowly for over a week,
suddenly burst into flames. A
message was sent to me in a way
which could be clearly heard by me.
It said, 'You touch that foreign woman
and then you are bold enough to go
about the house without a bath, with
only a change of clothes. We cannot
tolerate this. If you do not wish to
have a bath, you had better keep
yourself upstairs. Your food will be
sent there. You are turning yourself
into a 'madam' by learning English.
It would be only fitting to the pomp
of a 'madam' that she should have
her food upstairs. After all we are
here, downstairs, all the slaves and
servants of my lady!'"

Ramabai then took her cold baths
until she came down with a fever and
her husband intervened. But when

she gave a short speech in English to
a gathering of women, the older
women in the family scolded not
only Ramabai but also her husband.

"Tai Sasubai, her mother-in-law
started a harangue. It went on till
nine-thirty. My husband was rather
late that night. Taibai continued in
an angry strain even after he got
back. But by then, her fury had abated
somewhat. She said, 'People have
given up all sense of honor these
days. In the good old days, women
did not even come into the presence
of men, let alone talk to them.... They
would not even lift up their heads,
even if their necks became stiff. Were
they not the darlings of their
husbands? Did they not know love?
But now, this love has crossed all
limits. Wives must now sit close to
their husbands, as though their
clothes were knotted. They must read
and write like men. So far this reading
and writing has been going on inside
the house. But today even that
boundary has been crossed. Were
you not ashamed to see your wife
reading out in English in the
presence of two thousand people? In
the old days, people valued their
good name above all. Now things are
all changed.... For heaven's sake,
give up all this teaching English, at
least for the present. Give an inch to
these girls today and they will
demand a mile. If you do not keep
them within strict bounds, they will
become uncontrollable.'"[1]

But despite these family quarrels,
Ramabai Ranade did persist and did
become active in encouraging other
women's education. But women's
education today in India is still an
issue. Marriage want-ads do suggest
some change in attitude, a lesser
dowry may be taken if the bride is
educated. Her potential money-
earning is seen as a real advantage
to joint family income. India's number
of women in judgeships, and as

1. Ramabai Ranade, *Ranade: His Wife's*
Reminiscences, (Publications Division, Ministry of
Information; New Delhi: 1963) pp. 49, 79, 88-90.

engineers, compares favorably with Western nations.

One problem which still may exist, however, is represented by the literacy rates shown on the following charts:

Literacy Rates
percentage of total population

1971 Census[2]		1969 Census[3]	
India		United States	
Male	Female	Male	Female
39.5	18.7	98.9	99

Points To Consider

1. Many of the best known reformers for women in India have been men. Why might have this been the case?

2. In the Ranade reading, it is the older women who give her the hardest time. In what ways did her learning to read pose a threat to them?

3. In looking at the statistics on India and the U.S., realizing the difference in resources between the two countries, what generalizations might you suggest?

4. One of the problems with education for Indian women was finding an appropriate school for them. If you were given money to establish a school in India around 1900; what sort of school would you establish? What reasons would you give for your choice?

   A. School for elite women, English speaking so that they could become national leaders.

   B. Home economics school, stressing better child care and sanitation.

   C. School for untouchable women and widows to train for nursing or teaching so that they could support themselves.

   D. Co-educational school emphasizing general knowledge with a choice in subject matter and friends.

   E. School set up along strict Hindu lines, to go back to Vedic traditions and maintain the culture.

2. Report on the Status of Women, *Towards Equality: Report on the Status of Women*, (New Delhi: Government of India, 1944) p. 31.
3. *Statistical Abstracts of the U.S., 1976*, (Washington, D.C. Department of Commerce, 1976).

Chapter 6

Women in Twentieth Century India

Chapter Contents

A. Women in Power

In the 1960's, Vijaya Lakshmi Pandit pointed to India with pride. She pointed out that there were 55 women in positions of real political power in India. This number represented, she claimed, more women in roles of serious political strength than in any other nation. Other observers also remarked at the visibility of Indian women politicians: how they seemed to have gone *"from purdah to power"* in one generation.

The chart, *Women Leaders in India* gives something of the background of 10 of the women who were recognized in India between 1920 – 1970 as having major roles in reform and politics. Two questions seem raised about these women:

1. Did they represent a real change in roles of women throughout India?

2. Will India continue to lead the world in the number of women in political roles?

While the chart below will not answer these questions completely, after looking through the chart materials and *answering the questions below,* what would your thesis be as to the two questions raised above?

CHART ANALYSIS

1. Were these reformers from all geographical sections of India?

2. Many of the Indian male reformers came from various castes; the Nehrus were Brahmans, Gandhi was a Vaishyas,[1] Ambedkar represented the Untouchables, and Jennah was a Muslim. What generalizations might be made about the caste and religion represented by the women reformers?

3. Are there any similarities in family background that might have allowed these women to become involved in politics?

4. The U.S. women's suffrage movement began when American women became involved in another reform, the anti-slavery movement. The discrimination they saw in trying to help blacks led to an awareness of their own problems with discrimination. Look at the causes for the women in India being jailed:

   A. What seems to be the main reason for their imprisonment?

   B. Who is the only woman specifically jailed for women's rights protest?

5. How did these women fit this model of the typical Indian woman's life?

   A. Early marriage, all women *have* to marry.
   B. Marry in own caste, religion.
   C. Remain in household, don't travel.
   D. Have children. (See: Marriage)
   E. Widows do not remarry.

---

1. Third caste, after Brahman and Kshatriya.

6. What sorts of issues did these women generally concern themselves with? What issues are not in their realms of concern? (See: Kinds of Reform)

7. Two of these women were from other countries. Do you see anything in their backgrounds which might have made them particularly interested in Indians gaining independence from Great Britain?

After looking through the chart, give four or five qualities of most of these reformers which might be typical:

	Aruna Asaf Ali	Annie Besant	Margaret Cousins	Indira Nehru Gandhi	Rajkumari Amit Kaur
Dates		1847–1933	1878–1954	1917–	1886–1964
Family	Middle class. Educated in Catholic and Protestant schools.	Daughter of minister. Parents died early, schooled in Paris. ˙		Only child. Nehru family. Relatives all in national movement.	Only daughter. Educated in Sherborne Sch. for Girls. Uncle was a Maharajah. Mother a social-worker.
Area	Bengal (North India)	Born in England but of Irish background	Ireland	Allahabad (Northern India)	Karputhala (Punjab) North India
Religion	Hindu, converted to Muslim	Christian, athiest, later head of Theoso-phical Society[1]	Christian	Kashmiri Brahmins	Father became Christian
Marriage	To Muslim	To minister, divorced, two children. Did not remarry.	To Dr. Cousins, both came to India.	To Feraze Gandhi, a Parsi. Two sons, widowed, not remarried.	Father did not believe in early marriage. She never married.
Travel	None	Widely, in western and eastern hemispheres.	To India, 1915; To U.S., 1932; protesting Indian leaders imprisonment.	England to school–Oxford. Switzerland, Italy, later the world.	Educ. in Eng. travelled the world.
Prison	1930 Salt March.[2] 1932: Independence Man. fugitive with 5000 rupee reward 1942–45.	Arrested in England as socialist, 1917. In India for Home Rule agitation[3]	Ireland — agitating for women's rights. 1932: Indian Home Rule.	1942: "Quit India" Movement.[4]	1932, arrested Salt Campaign; 1937, arrested Ind. Movement 1942: "Quit India"
Kinds of Reform	India Independ. Improving prison conditions.	Irish national movement, untouchables, Hindu language schools, Home Rule, ed. for women.	Women's rights Irish Women's League. Independence for India. Untouchables.	Indian independ. Women's rights. Untouchables.	Health. Indian Independence. Sanitation.
Achievements	Underground leader, publisher, editor. Mayor of Delhi 1958. Gandhi organ. non-violent protest on Brit. monopoly & taxing salt.	1917: Pres. India National Congress. Founded Hindu College. Schools for girls. Started Home Rule League. Pres. International Theosophical Society.	Founded Women's India Association. Pushed and helped get vote for India women, 1933.	1959: Pres. of Congress Party 1964: Minister of Inform. and Broadcasting. 1967: Prime Minister. (Third generation grandfather and father had been pres. of Cong. Party also.)	Introduced women's sports. Sec. & Pres. All Indian Women Conference. Minister of Health. President of International Red Cross.

2. Theosophical Society is a religion blending Eastern and Western ideas. Stresses reincarnation and passages of life through time.

3. Gandhi organized non-violent protest on British monopoly and taxing of salt.

Points To Consider

1. Do you think the woman represented by the qualities you chose in question no. 7, p. 92 would be typical of Indian women generally? Why, or why not?

2. Based on your answer above, what prediction would you have for the future involvement of women in Indian politics?

3. Looking back to the original two questions at the beginning of the exercise, what is your thesis or opinion concerning these questions?

Muthulakshmi Reddi	Vijaya Lakshmi (Nehru) Pandit	Pandita Ramabai	Ramabai Ranade	Sarojini Naidu
1886	1900	1855–1922	1862–1922	1879–1949
Middle class. She was given education.	Eldest daughter Motilal Nehru. Member of revolutionary family. Educated at home.	Father/Mother were Sanskrit scholars. She was educated Parents and brother died of starvation in famine.	Traditional Hindu family. No formal education in home. Married at eleven. Educated by husband.	Father was a physician. Educated at Univ. Madras & Kings College, England.
Madras (Southern India)	Allahabad (Northern India)	Northern India	Bombay area (Central India)	Bengal, Hyderabad (North India)
	Kashmiri Brahmans	Orthodox Brahmin, later converted Christianity.	Brahmin	Bengal; Brahmans
To Narayana Sastri	To Ranjit Pandit (Third Caste) 1921, two daughters, widowed, did not remarry.	In 1880 to low-caste Bengali, one daughter, widowed in 1882, never remarried.	To Brahmin reformer who taught her to read/write. Three children, widowed, never remarried.	To Govidurhajul Naidu (Third caste Hindu) Four children.
England, 1920's to study women's ed. 1933 to U.S., England	Various trips to Europe, then throughout the world.	To. U.S., England to see social services programs.	In India	Cambridge, England, 1924; S. Africa. 1923–29; tours to U.S.
1932: boycott of foreign cloth.	1921: boycott Prince Edward's visit. 1932: Home Rule. 1940-42 — "Quit India Movement"[6]	None	None	1921: boycott Prince Edward's visit. 1930: Salt March. 1940-42 "Quit India Movement"
Avvi Home for destitutes. Leg. to end Devadasis. Women's rights. Handicapped.	Health, education, India's independence.	Widow's homes. Famine relief.	Widow relief. Public health.	Women's rights (England). Indian self rule. Hindu: Muslim unity.
First woman in legislature, first Deputy Pres. of Leg. Council. First woman grad. Medical School of Madras. Founded Cancer Hospital.	Chairman of Education Com. Rep. United Prov. Assembly. First woman Pres. of U. N. Gen. Assembly. Ambassador to U. S., U. S. S. R.	Scholar Founded societies to educate women. Homes for high caste widows.	Hindu Lady's Club. Founded widow's home in Poona. Started nursing & med. assoc. for women. Wrote autobiography considered minor "classic."	Major poet of India. "Nightingale of India." 1924: President India Congress. Governor of Ultar Pradesh (Indian state).

4. Desire for India to gain commonwealth rights.
5. Movement during World War II to force British out of India.

6. Protest against his coming, part of Home Rule movement.

**Indira Gandhi:
Prime Minister of India**

(Wide World Photo)

**Vijaya Lakshmi Pandit,
President of
United Nations Assembly**

Annie Besant: President
of India National
Congress, 1917

Sarojini Naidu:
President of India
National Congress, 1924

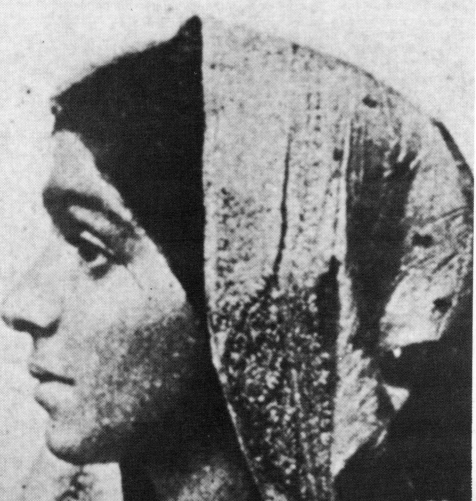

B. Women in Contemporary India

Indian women, like women in many other nations, are caught between two processes. One of these is the industrializing and urbanizing shift of population from an agrarian village community. The other process is one of nationalism and concern for the preservation of heritage and national ideals. For Indian women this conflict in values may be seen in many of their writings on women's liberation. They see the modern women's rights movement as coming from the west and being foreign to Indian ideals. Often they criticize the movement as "making women into men" and forgetting that women have a special role as mother. For example, Dr. Pratima Asthana, a college professor and President of the Women's Association of Agra, claims that "by nature and temperament a woman is at her best and happiest when she is the director of a household. She is a mother first and last."[1] This ideal of motherhood is one deeply ingrained in the Indian culture.

Yet, other writers see the future of Indian women as *both* directors of households and as college professors. However, maintaining the two roles of career woman and housewife/mother can lead to difficulties. A small group of Indian women are trying to have both the "western ideal" of a career while also fulfilling the expectations of the Indian religious and cultural ideals of perfect wife and mother. In a recent study an Indian sociologist, Promilla Kapur, pointed out that this mixture of the "modern" ideal of independent career woman with the Indian ideal of a submissive, all devoted wife and mother has created conflict in some marriages. This is especially true when the husband does not approve of his wife working.[2] Also, since few Indian men are used to household work, Indian working women tend to be over-worked by their double duty.

The following figures suggest the employment rate for women in India:

Working Women in India: 1971 Census

Rural

13% of women working
87% in agriculture
 2% in industry

Urban

7% of women working
38% in service jobs
17.5% in agriculture
13% in industry[3]

1. Pratima Asthana, *Women's Movement in India* (Delhi: Vikas Publishing House Prt., Ltd., 1974) p. 158.
2. Promilla Kapur, *Marriage and the Working Woman* (Delhi: Vikas Publishing House Prt., Ltd., 1970), pp. 438-439.
3. Quoted by Ashish Bose, "A Demographic Profile," Devaki Jain, (ed) *Indian Women*, (New Delhi: Ministry of Information and Broadcasting: 1975), p. 133.

Woman construction worker

Notice that the rate of employment of women is low. The term "working women" is, of course, a difficult one because statistical figures do not count household work as "work." Another problem with such statistics is that most low caste women are field workers but are not always counted as "agricultural workers." India is still a nation of villages: 70% of her people live in small, rural villages. While changes have occurred for many women, reforms for village women have come very slowly.

But even middle class women of India seem to have mixed ideas about change. The following concerns a 1976 study of working women's attitudes in both Turkey and India. Both of these countries are slowly going through the process called "modernization." In other words, from being traditional agricultural countries they are becoming urbanized and industrialized. The study revealed some interesting things about working, educated women in India. The following data is taken from this study.[4]

1. In both Turkey and India the traditional decisions about marriage partners of children were made by the parents. Marriages were arranged by parents rather than by individual choice of young people. One would hypothesize that as women became more modernized they would wish to choose their own husbands. Here are the results of the study:

Turkey		India
32.8%	wished parents to choose husband	74.2%
(not included in questionnaire)	Indifferent	7.5%
67.%	did **not** wish parents to choose husband	18.3%

2. Also, traditional Indian society was based on a complex caste system. One would hypothesize that as women became more modern they would favor inter-caste marriage. Here is the result of the question:

"Inter-caste Marriages Should Not Take Place"

55%	Against statement (all right to have inter-caste marriages)
12.5%	Indifferent
32.5%	Believed inter-caste marriages should *not* take place.[5]

What was the percentage of young women in Turkey who did *not* want an arranged marriage? _____
In India? _____

What aspects of Indian society might make even modern girls reluctant to give up arranged marriages? How would this perhaps partly relate to the second set of figures on inter-caste marriages?

In looking at Indian women and the future they see for themselves, it may be best to look at what they see as some of their own goals. In 1973 the Government of India set up a committee to study the status of Indian women. The report of this committee was published in 1975.

Among their recommendations for needed reforms in Indian laws and customs were the following suggestions:[6]

1. *A campaign to educate Indian women about their legal rights.* Although many laws have been passed that benefit women they are often ignorant about them because of strong local customs and low female literacy.

4. Raj Mohini Sethi, *Modernization of Working Women in Developing Societies* (New Delhi: National Publication House, 1976), pp. 67, 73, 82.
5. *Ibid.*, p. 73.
6. *Towards Equality: Report of the Committee on the Status of Women in India* (New Delhi: Government of India, 1974), pp. 359-364.

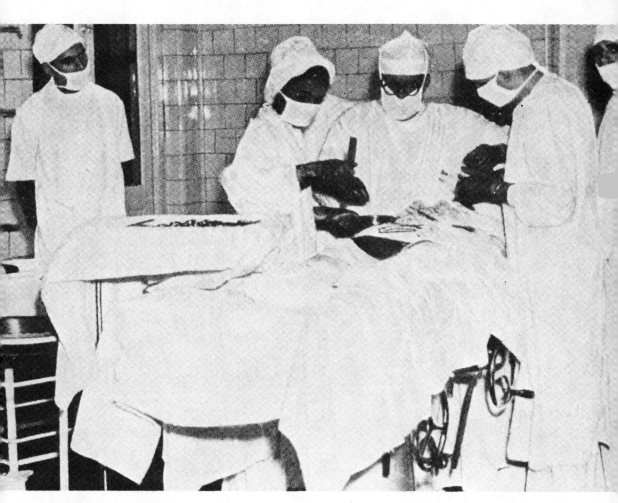

Woman surgeon

2. *That the age of marriage for girls be raised from 15 to 18.* Also, that the present law be enforced as many girls are still married before 15 especially in rural India. The committee attributes the high suicide rate among young Indian girls to early marriage. Also, they discovered that 18% of adult Indians still believe strongly in child (pre-puberty) marriage.

3. *Get rid of polygyny in Muslim law.* Muslim Indians are still allowed to have more than one wife.

4. *Improve divorce laws.* Divorce laws should be liberalized -- still very long and difficult process that works mostly against Indian women.

5. *That more vigorous measures be taken to get rid of dowrys.* A 1961 law was meant to outlaw dowrys but has failed because it allowed unlimited "gifts." A limit of the values of gifts and a prohibition against displaying the gifts was suggested.

6. *Extending maternity benefits to groups of women not covered.* This is a controversial suggestion because some observers feel that maternity benefits have increased the birth rate.

7. *Setting up of day care centers (or 'creches') for the children of working women.* Many poor women work as laborers and their babies have to be brought with them.

8. *Equalization of wages.* A law guaranteeing "equal pay for equal work."

9. *Coeducation and universal education to age 14.* Wherever possible coeducation, but all girls provided with free education to age 14.

10. *Part time jobs and retraining programs for women who have been out of the job market.* Some provisions for women who need to spend more time working for their families -- more flexibility.

Points To Consider

1. Which of these reforms would not be necessary in a country like the United States?

2. Which would seem to be a goal any nation committed to equality of the sexes might have?

3. Which, based on your knowledge of Indian culture, would you see as one that really should be stressed?

4. Would the changes suggested be merely "tinkering" with the social system in India or would it result in deeper social changes that would cause widespread economic or religious changes?

Selected Bibliography

NON-FICTION

*Altekar, A. S. *The Position of Women in Hindu Civilization.* Banaras: Motilal Banarsidass, 1956.

Baig, Tara Ali, *India's Woman Power,* New Delhi: S. Chand & Co., Ltd., 1976.

Bullough, Vern L., *The History of Prostitution.* New Hyde Park, New York: University Books, 1964.

Cooke, David. *Dera: A Village in India.* New York: W. W. Norton Co., 1967.

De Souza, Alfred, ed. *Women in Contemporary India.* Delhi: Ramesh C. Jain, 1975.

Dube, S. C. *Indian Village.* New York: Harper, Row Colophon Books, 1967.

Dubey, Dinesh and Anita Bardham, *Status of Women and Fertility in India.* New Delhi, National Institute of Family Planning, 1972.

Gandhi, M. K. *Women and Social Justice.* Ahmedabad: Narajiran Publishing House, 1942.

*Gupta, Giri Raj: *Marriage, Religion and Society.* Delhi: Vikas Publishing House, Pvt., Ltd., 1974.

Hate, Chandrakala A., *Changing Status of Woman.* Bombay: Allied Publishers Private, Limited, 1969.

Jacobson, Doranne and Susan Wadley. *Women in India -- Two Perspectives.* New Delhi: Manohar, 1977.

*Jain, Devaki, ed., *Indian Women.* New Delhi: Ministry of Information and Broadcasting, 1975.

Kapur, Promilla, *Marriage and the Working Woman in India.* Delhi: Vikas Publishing House, Private, Ltd., 1974.

Kaur, Manmohan. *Role of Women in the Freedom Movement.* (1857-1947). Delhi: Sterling Publishers Private, Ltd., 1968.

Khan, Mazhar ul Haq. *Purdah and Polygamy.* Peshawar: Nashiran e Ilin o Taraqiyet, 1972.

Lannoy, Richard, *The Speaking Tree: A Study of Indian Culture and Society.* New York: Oxford U. Press, 1971.

Lewis, Oscar. *Village Life in Northern India,* New York: Vintage Books, Random House, Inc., 1965.

Mandelbaum, David G. *Human Fertility in India.* Berkeley: University of California Press, 1974.

Mehta, Rama. *The Western Educated Hindu Woman*. New York: Asia Publishing House, 1970.

*Minturn, Leigh and John T. Hitchcock, *The Rajputs of Kalapur, India*, Six Culture Series, Vol. 3, New York: John Wiley and Sons, 1966.

*Nanda, B. R. *Indian Women: From Purdah to Modernity*. New Delhi: Vikas Publishing House, PVT., LTD., 1976.

Roy, Beth. *Bullock Carts and Motorbikes*. New York: Atheneum, 1972.

Roy, Manisha. *Bengali Woman*. Chicago: University of Chicago Press, 1972.

Sethi, Raj Mohini, *Modernization of Working Women in Developing Societies.*. New Delhi: National Publishing House, 1976.

Shrideri, S. *Gandhi and the Emancipation of Indian Women*. Hyderabad: Gandhi: Schithy s Prachuranalycyam, 1969.

Thomas, P. *Incredible India*. Bombay: D. B. Taraporevala Sons, 1966.

Towards Equality: Report of the Committee on the Status of Women in India. New Delhi: Government of India, Department of Social Welfare, Ministry of Education and Social Welfare, 1974.

Ordering Information: Department of Social Welfare, Government of India, New Delhi Printed at: Printing Press Institute for the Deaf, 4 E. 16 Jhandewalan Extension, New Delhi 110055.

Vatick, Sylvia. *Kinship of Urbanization*. Berkeley: University of California Press, 1972.

*Vreede, DeStuers, Cora. *Parda: A Study of Muslim Women's Life in Northern India*. Assen, Netherlands: Van Gorcum & Comp., 1968.

Wolpert, Stanley. *A New History of India*. (Best general history that includes women) New York: Oxford University Press, 1977.

Wiser, William and Charlotte. *Behind Mud Walls*, 1930-1960. Berkeley: University of California Press, 1964.

FICTION

*Desai, Anita. *Fire on the Mountain*. New York: Harper and Row, 1978.

Jhabrala, R. Prawer. *Like Birds, Like Fishes, and Other Stories*. New York: W. W. Norton & Co., Inc., 1963.

Markandaya, Kamala. *Nectar in a Sieve*. New York: John Day, 1955.

Mukherjee, Bharat: *The Tiger's Daughter*. Boston: Houghton Mifflin Co., 1971.

Premchand, *The Chess Players and Other Stories*, Trans., Gurdial Mallik. Delhi: Hind Pocket Books, 1967.

Premchand, *The Gift of a Cow*. Bloomington: Indiana University Press, 1967.

Premchand, *The Shroud and 20 Other Stories*. New Delhi: Sagar Publications, 1972.

*Premchand. *The World of Premchand*. Trans., David Rubin. Bloomington, Indiana University Press, 1909.

Rav Santha Rama. *Remember the House*. New York: Harper, Bros., 1956.

*Strauss, Carolyn. *Earth Below, Heaven Above*. New York: Scribner's, 1972.

Tandon, Pradash, *Punjabi Century: 1857-1957*. Berkeley: University of California Press, 1968.

ART

Ghosh, Dena Prasad. *Kama ratna: Indian Ideals of Feminine Beauty*. New Delhi: R & K: Pub. House, 1973.

Mehta, Rustam. *Masterpieces of the Female Form in Indian Art*. Bombay: D. B. Taraporevala Sons & Co. Private, Ltd., 1972.

Mode, Heinz. *Women in Indian Art*. Leipzig: (GDR), 1970.

BIOGRAPHY — AUTOBIOGRAPHY

Bhatia, Krishen. *Indira, Biography of Prime Minister Indira Gandhi*. New York: Praeger, 1974.

Baig, Tara Ali. *Sarojini Naidu*. Delhi: Publications Division, Government of India, 1975. (Biography)

Andrews, Robert Hardy. *A Lamp for India: The Story of Madame Pandit*. London: Arthur Barker Ltd., 1967.

*Felton, Monica. *A Child Widow's Story*. London: Victor Gollancz Ltd., 1966.

*Ikramullah, Shaista S., *From Purdah to Parliament*, London: The Cresset Press, 1963.

Karve, Dinakar D., Trans., *The New Brahmans, Five Maharashtrian Families*. Berkeley: University of California Press, 1963.

Ishvani, *The Brocaded Sari*. New York: John Day Co., 1946.

*Mazumdar, Shudha. *A Pattern of Life: the Memoirs of an Indian Woman*. New Delhi: Ramesh C. Jain, 1977

*Mehta, Ved. *Mamaji*. New York: Oxford University Press, 1979.

Morton, Eleanor. *Women Behind Mahatma Gandhi*. London: Max Reinhardt Stellar Press, 1954.

Nanda, Sanitri. *The City of Two Gateways: The Autobiography of an Indian Girl*. London: G. Allen & Unwin, 1950.

Pandit, Vijayalakshmi. *Prison Days*. Calcutta: Signet Press, 1943.

Sahgal, Nayantara. *Prison and Chocolate Cake*. New York: Knopf, 1954.

*Starred items are particularly valuable sources.

Glossary

Aryans: Invaders from Central Europe who conquered North India between 1500–500 B.C.

Bai: Maharshtra (one of the local languages of India) word meaning woman.

Bande Mataram: "Hail to the Mother"; the first Indian national anthem.

Brahaminas: Women in Vedic times who remained unmarried and spent their lives studying the Vedas.

Brahman: Hindu priests; the first or highest caste (today not all Brahmins are priests).

Bride Price: The same as a dowry but reverse: money, goods or land are paid by the husband to bride's family.

Caste: An Indian social group whose members intermarry, will eat together, and are bound together by the same ritual laws of Hinduism. Often, but not always, related to occupation.

Devadasi: "Slave of God"; used to describe girls devoted to the temple as dancers (and later as prostitutes).

Devi: A great Hindu female God.

Diversity: Wide variety or variations.

Dowry: Payment in money, goods, or land, to the future husband or his family by the bride's family.

Durga: A female Hindu usually pictured as a warrior.

Ghee: Butter cooked down to oil (this oil is called ghee) used in Indian cooking but also in some Hindu ceremonies.

Gotra=Clan: Group that traces lineage to a single ancestor -- in India of the male line.

Harijans= "Child of God": Mahatma Gandhi's name for untouchables. The four varnas or castes are above them -- although they are sometimes included with the Sudra caste. Untouchables do the most lowly tasks that other Hindus will not do: sweeping, cleaning bathrooms, and tanning leather.

Hierarchy: A system of persons or things *ranked* one above the other.

Jati:	Sub-castes; usually made up of people of like occupation, people who marry each other, etc. Like "caste;" very complex to define; thousands of jati or sub-castes in India.
Joint Family:	Practice whereby a group of people with a common male ancestor live together, share economic resources, tasks, and living space.
Kanya:	Virgin Bride; Kanyadan a ceremony, part of wedding, giving of the bride as a present.
Kshatriya:	Hindu warrior; second highest caste.
Kunku:	Red powder mark on forehead of unmarried girls and women whose husbands are living.
Levirate:	Marriage of a widow to her dead husband's brother. Common in ancient times for reasons of inheritance and family name.
Mantras:	Hindu prayers from the Vedas.
Mohalla:	A suburban neighborhood or residential area of a village.
Niyoga:	Sometimes seen as the Indian form of levirate marriage; sometimes the widow has a child by her dead husband's brother without formal marriage.
Orthodox:	Strict following of religious laws.
Palanquin or Doli:	A box-like enclosure used to carry women in purdah on errands outside their homes. Servants carry it on poles placed on their shoulders.
Pativrata:	The ideal Hindu wife: devoted to her husband, self sacrificing loyal and submissive.
Polyandry:	The practice of allowing women to have several husbands at the same time.
Polygamy:	Having several spouses at the same time.
Polygyny:	The practice of having more than one wife at a time.
Purdah:	Confining of women and separating them from men. Women are given special places inside to live; outside they wear veils over their faces and clothes that completely cover them.
Rajput:	Members of Kshatriya caste from Rajasthan in Northwest India. During the middle ages were the "Prince Kings" who ruled small kingdoms and were known as fierce warriors.
Rigveda (or Rgveda):	The early, holy "books" of Hinduism. These were hymns and prayers of the Aryans who invaded India between c. 1500–500 B.C. The Rigveda was not written down until recently. It was passed along orally (memorized and spoken).

Risis: Women who composed Vedic hymns; female poets in ancient times.

Rite of Passage: Ceremonies, common in many cultures, to initiate young people to adulthood. (In U.S., church confirmation or bas/bar mitzvah might be examples.)

Samana: Festival or fair of Vedic times. Women and girls were allowed to attend these festivals and met potential mates there.

Sanskritization: Lower castes or sub-castes copying customs of higher castes in an attempt to rise in status.

Sati (Suttee): Self immolation (burning) of a widow on her husband's funeral pyre. Actually the word refers to the person and means "true one" but has come to mean true act.

Shakti: Female power, the active force in Hinduism.

Stridhana: The jewelry and personal belongings that a bride takes with her into a marriage. These possessions cannot be taken from her and are her security in case of trouble. However, very often they are used to help the family and not saved for the woman's use.

Sudras: Lowest caste, women are often equated to Sudras because both are not allowed to read, study, or say the Vedas.

"Twiceborn" Castes (DWIJ): Highest castes; spiritual rebirth -- boys undergo upnayan or the "string ritual" (janeu).

Vaisya: Third caste from the top; a "twice born" caste -- traditionally the merchant caste.

Varna: The four major castes (from top to bottom): Brahmin, Kshatriya, Vaisya, and Sudra. According to the Rigveda the four castes came from the body of the great God, Purush -- the Brahmin from the mouth, the Kshatriya from the arms, the Vaisya from the thighs, and Sudra from the feet. Untouchables are classed beneath the Sudras or with them.

Vedas: The oral hymns and prayers that are the basis of Hinduism. Composed by the Aryans between 1500 B.C.-500 B.C.

Vratas: Vows, fasts, rites performed by women. Women are not allowed to say the Vedas so these prayers, etc., are especially for them.

Zenana: The part of a Hindu (or Indian Muslim) home reserved for women.

Chronology

POLITICAL CHRONOLOGY, 2500 B.C. - 1977

c. 2500-1500 B.C.
Indus Valley Civilization
(Mahenjo Daro and Harappa, the two major cities) High civilization, signs of written language, trade

Since Indus Valley language has not been translated, there is only archaeological evidence

c. 1500-500 B.C.: VEDIC AGE
"Aryan" invasions from Central Europe; Aryans conquer and spread over North India; Vedas composed

c. 567 B.C. BUDDHA IS BORN
A reformer of Hinduism, Buddha starts preaching in c. 532 B.C.

c. 327 B.C.: Alexander the Great
Briefly conquers northern India, leaving Greek generals and culture behind when he leaves (dies 323 B.C.)

c. 305–232 B.C. MAURYAN DYNASTY
Chandragupta conquers and consolidates North India into Mauryan Empire
(Epic poem *Mahabharata* composed in c. 300 B.C.)
Ramayana

Chandragupta's minister writes *Arthashastra*

c. 265 B.C. Ashoka (or Asoka) The Great becomes Mauryan emperor

261 B.C. Ashoka converts to Buddhism

WOMEN'S CHRONOLOGY, 2500 B.C. – 1977

c. 2500-1500 B.C.
Indus Valley Civilization
Prevalence of mother Goddesses, dancing girls, well-organized life

c. 1500-500 B.C. VEDIC AGE
Aryan women marry at about 16 (after puberty), take part in religion, are allowed physical freedom
Widows remarry and girls have some choice about marriage partners

Status: High, except for area of inheritance

c. 530 B.C.: Buddha reluctantly allows women into church as nuns, many women join Buddhist monasteries; discrimination against them, but for a few hundred years, are Buddhist nuns

c. 300 B.C. - 500 A.D.
PERIOD OF STATUS DECLINE
Women's position over this 800-year period shows a general decline: See "Status of Widows." 316 B.C.: First historical sati; a few cases of sati in poem; mostly an ideal child marriage; beginning of sati; some seclusion of women; deprived of physical freedom; lack of education; lose right to say Vedas

Women retain some rights and marriage choices in Arthashastra

Ashoka's wife probably converted him to Buddhism and encouraged his "Law of Righteousness"

Ashoka's daughter, Sanghamitra, became a Buddhist preacher-nun in Ceylon.

232 B.C. - 320 A.D.: Period of Invasion and Disorder	**Women's status continues to decline;** perhaps disorder contributes to need to protect and restrict women
	Manu's Laws developed in this period -- codified in c. 100 A.D. Some veiling of upper class women
320-467: The Gupta Dynasty Chandragupta I Samudragupta Chandragupta II	
c. 500 "Puranas" or folk tales given present form	Puranas mention only a few cases of sati
467-606: Invasions and Disunity ("White Huns")	**c. 500: Bhakti Religious Sect** -- Poets Bhakti attracts women because of mystical achievement of Moksha
	Sati becoming customary among warriors, leaders. **c. 510:** General Goparaja dies fighting Huns. Widow commits sati
606-647: King Harsha briefly unites northern India	**606:** Mother of King Harsha commits sati on death of husband King Harsha prevents sisters from sati
	c. 625: Poet Bana writes against sati, Tantric sect writers also oppose sati
c. 700: North India, Rajput Kingdoms (dominated north for 1,000 years) small, warrior kingdoms -- disunity in north continues	**c. 700-1100: Sati is supported and glorified** in writing; becomes frequent in North Indian high castes
	May have had some signs of beginnings of purdah
1100-1524: Period of Invasion and Disunity **c. 1400: Timur (Tamerlane)** sacks Delhi **c. 1498: Vasco de Gama** arrives at Goa	**1100-1524: Sati becomes ideal** for women of upper castes (lower castes tend to imitate)
	Purdah, in imitation of Muslims, comes into style among upper castes/rich
1524-1707: **PERIOD OF GREAT MUSLIM EMPIRES** Babur **1556-1605: Akbar's Empire** **1658-1707: Aurargzeb's Empire**	**1556-1605:** Akbar speaks out against child marriage, tries to stamp out sati, has little success

1700-1764: British East India Company gains North India (Bengal)

1764-1858: British East India Company "rules" North India with some Parliamentary controls

1857: Sepoy Rebellion

1858: Queen crowned Empress of India. British government takes control from British East India Company

1930: Salt March

1941: "Quit India" Movement

1947: India/Pakistan gain independence. Jawaharlal Nehru is first Prime Minister

1948: Gandhi is assassinated

1966: Indira Gandhi becomes Prime Minister of India

1700-1829: British disapproving of "native" customs like sati, but keep to policy of hands off

1829: Sir William Bentinck prohibits sati in Bengal (British India)

1856: British pass Widow Remarriage Act. Angers Indians as act of British interference with Hindu customs -- one cause of Sepoy Rebellion

1858-1884: Period of British non-intervention -- child marriage, illegal sati, problem of widows continue

1884: Beginnings of Indian women's voluntary organizations

1885: Indian National Congress formed

1909: "Seva Sadan" -- Ranade starts women's training school (Annie Besant first president)

1919-1947: Women came out from purdah to work for Independence Movement; especially Gandhi

1920: Madras -- National Council of Women of India

1929: "Sarda Act" ends child marriage by law

1931: Women promised the vote. In 1935, government of India Act extends franchise to some Indian women

1966: Indira Gandhi becomes Prime Minister of India

June 13, 1975: Indira Gandhi found guilty of unfair campaign tactics -- starts "emergency" measures on June 26, 1975, to stay in power

1977: Indira Gandhi ends emergency measures -- loses election to Desai

February 1977: Morarji Desai becomes Prime Minister after his "Janata" Party defeats Indira's Congress Party

1980: Desai loses elections

October 1977: Indira Gandhi arrested in India. Later released

1980: Indira Gandhi again becomes Prime Minister of India

About The Authors

Majorie Wall Bingham was born in Nebraska and received her B.A. Degree from Grinnell College and her M.A. and Ph.D. Degrees from the University of Minnesota. Her teaching experience includes being a junior high school teacher in Davenport, Iowa and an instructor at the University of Minnesota. Currently she is teaching history in the St. Louis Park, Minnesota, schools. Her professional activities include being a member of the Minnesota Council for the Social Studies Executive Board, on the Education Board of the Minnesota Historical Society and President of WHOM (Women Historians of the Midwest).

Susan Hill Gross was born in Minnesota and received her B.A. Degree from the University of Minnesota and her M.A. Degree in History from the College of William and Mary. Ms. Gross taught secondary English and history in Denbigh, Virginia, Savannah, Georgia and the Robbinsdale Schools in Minnesota before becoming a director of the curriculum project Women In World Area Studies. She served on the Robbinsdale Central Committee for student affairs, as treasurer of the Minnesota Council for the Social Studies and is presently recorder for WHOM (Women Historians of the Midwest).

Dr. Bingham and Ms. Gross have been invited frequently to lecture to various educational and community groups on issues concerning women's history, integrating women's studies into the curriculum and on issues concerning Title IX.